LOVING in TRUTH

ALSO BY JAY ROGOFF

BOOKS of POETRY

Enamel Eyes, A Fantasia on Paris, 1870

Venera

The Art of Gravity

The Long Fault

How We Came to Stand on That Shore

The Cutoff: A Sequence (Washington Prize for Poetry)

CHAPBOOKS and LIMITED EDITIONS

Twenty Danses Macabres (Robert Watson Poetry Award)

Venera (artist's book by Kate Leavitt with her original intaglio prints)

First Hand (John Masefield Award)

NEW AND SELECTED POEMS

LOVING in TRUTH

Jay Rogoff

LOUISIANA STATE UNIVERSITY PRESS
BATON ROUGE

Published with the assistance of the Sea Cliff Fund

Published by Louisiana State University Press
Copyright © 2020 by Jay Rogoff
All rights reserved
Manufactured in the United States of America
First printing

DESIGNER: Mandy McDonald Scallan
TYPEFACE: Adobe Caslon Pro
PRINTER AND BINDER: LSI

Library of Congress Cataloging-in-Publication Data
Names: Rogoff, Jay, author.
Title: Loving in truth : new and selected poems / Jay Rogoff.
Description: Baton Rouge : Louisiana State University Press, [2020]
Identifiers: LCCN 2019047546 (print) | LCCN 2019047547 (ebook) | ISBN 978-0-8071-7204-9 (paperback) | ISBN 978-0-8071-7352-7 (pdf) | ISBN 978-0-8071-7353-4 (epub)
Subjects: LCGFT: Poetry.
Classification: LCC PS3568.O486 L68 2020 (print) | LCC PS3568.O486 (ebook) | DDC 811/.54—dc23
LC record available at https://lccn.loc.gov/2019047546
LC ebook record available at https://lccn.loc.gov/2019047547

The paper in this book meets the guidelines for permanence and durability of the Committee on Production Guidelines for Book Longevity of the Council on Library Resources. ∞

For Ellie, Teo, Joey, Ben, and Katie

Therefore all seasons shall be sweet to thee . . .

CONTENTS

Acknowledgments 13

From *How We Came to Stand on That Shore* (2003)
    Seltzer 3
    Visions of Great-Grandmother 5
    Welcome to the Family 7
    Did the Black-and-White Movies Make My Mother? 9
    My Mother's Studio Apartment 10
    The Planes Came Home to the Airport 11
    How We Came to Stand on That Shore 12
    Good Night 13
    From "First Hand" 14
    The Rock and Roll Angel 19
    Strown Bliss, Scattering Bright 20
    The Vintage 21
    Awakening 22
    A Ghost 23
    Driving in Fog 24

From *The Cutoff: A Sequence* (1995)
    In the Box 27
    Aesthetics 29
    Sacrifice 31
    Extra Innings 33
    The Slide 35
    Everything but Everything 37

From *Venera* (2014)
> Courtship at Isenheim 41
> The Kindergarten Heart 43
> Adirondack Scenic 45
> Dazzle 46
> Life Sentence 47
> Dirty Linen 49
> Only Child 50
> Laughter 52

From "Venera"
> The Reader 56
> The Mother 56
> The Light 57
> The Sister 57
> The Field 58
> The Ark 58
> The Handmaid 59
> The House 59
> The Earth 60
> The Fountain 60
> The Garden 61
> The Singer 61
> The Bride 62
> The Mirror 62
> The Table 63
> The Lover 63

From *The Art of Gravity* (2011)
> Invocation 67
> Museum 69
> Latin Class 71
> Serenade 73

Scenery 75
Rehearsal in Summer 77
Adagio 79
Exuberance 80
Mid-Air 81
The Lesson of Orpheus 82
Translated 85
Dance of the Snowflakes 86
Making a Fool of Myself over Maria Kowroski 89
Sonnambula 91

From "Danses Macabres"
    Death Goes to a Party 94
    Death's Comfort 94
    Sweet Decorum 95
    Matter of Death 95
    Horoscope 96
    Death Makes the Man 96
    Death the Dietician 97
    Death's Theater 97
    Death's Addiction 98
    Death's Animation 98
    Death Sings Lieder 99
    La Valse 99
    Last Dance 100
    Death's Love 100
    Death in Disguise 101
    Death the Mother 101
    Death in the Woods 102
    Reception 102
    Breathless 103
    Death at Midnight 103
    Curtain Call 104
    Envoy: Come Away, Death 104

From *The Long Fault* (2008)
    Tempera 107
    Sublimated 108
    Book Burning 109
    Aspirations 112
    Folding the Flag 113
    The Guy Who Passed Me Doing 90 MPH and
        Playing the Trumpet 114
    Looking Out 115
    Nether Stowey 117
    Jane Austen, Inventor of Baseball 118
    Absorption 119
    In Camera 120
    The Golden Chamber 122
    Mennonites by the Sea 125
    A Breakdown 126
    The Collapse 127
    Such Stuff 128
    Carmelite Convent, Mexico DF 130
    Memorial Chapel 132
    The Hildesheim Doors 134
    Three Women 136
    The Old and New Cemeteries 138
    Poets' Park, Mexico DF 141

From *Enamel Eyes, A Fantasia on Paris, 1870* (2016)
    Wing Light 145
    Swanilda Waltzes 147
    The Emperor Attends *Coppélia* 149
    The Creator's Love for His Creation 150
    Coppélia Tells the Facts of Life 153
    Giuseppina Gets a Lesson in Courtship 155
    Swanilda Arms for War 157
    Ends of Empire 158

Votive Offerings 160
Travesty 162
Daughters of Invention 164
Swanilda Meets Her Twin 165
Just Looking 166
A Debate about Realism 167
Fever Dream 169
Festival of the Bells 170
Le Jardin des Tuileries 171
Seventeen at Last 172

Loving in Truth: *New Poems*

1. The Penny Poems
   All the Same 175
   Musing 176
   The Garden 177
   Holes in the Picture 178
   Dyeing 179
   The Good Death 180
   January 181
   Corpus Christi 182
   A New Lover 183
   Penny and the Bear 184
   Tortugas 185
   The Protestant Cemetery 186
   Punta Marina 187
   Research Assistant 188
   Penny Mourns the Raspberries 189
   Stragglers 190
   Legacy 191
   Double Waking 192
   At the War Museum 193
   Birthday in Middle Age 194
   Old Snapshots 195

2. Side Issue
    Beginning 197
    Chaos Theory 199
    Day Five 200
    Foresight 202
    Open Heart 203
    Side Issue 205
    Temptation 207
    In Hiding 209
    Fall 211
    End of the Affair 213
    Death's Sympathy 214
    Cain's Gift 215

3. Loving in Truth
    In the King's Arms 216
    The Little Black Boy 218
    First Negative 219
    Time Out 220
    The Buried Future 221
    One-Liner 222
    Higher Criticism 223
    Waking to the *Enigma Variations* 224
    My Computer Reads Me a Poem 225
    Witness 226
    The Wilton Diptych 227
    Consumption 228
    Manhattan 229
    Wear 230

About the Author 231

ACKNOWLEDGMENTS

Most poems in this book appeared in earlier collections. I am grateful to the Word Works for permission to reprint poems from *The Cutoff: A Sequence* (1995), published as winner of the Washington Prize for Poetry, and to River City Publishing for permission to reprint poems from *How We Came to Stand on That Shore* (2003).

I owe thanks to the editors of the journals where the following new poems first appeared, many in earlier forms: *Able Muse:* "Musing" and "Temptation"; *Agenda:* "All the Same"; *Agenda* (online edition): "Open Heart"; *Chautauqua Literary Journal:* "End of the Affair" and "Foresight"; *Confrontation:* "Day Five"; *Epoch:* "The Good Death"; *Field:* "January" and "Tortugas"; *Green Mountains Review:* "The Buried Future"; *The Grove Review:* "Time Out"; *The Hopkins Review:* "At the War Museum" and "Double Waking"; *Hotel Amerika:* "Chaos Theory" and "Holes in the Picture" (as "Holes in the Painting"); *The Hudson Review:* "First Negative"; *The Journal:* "Wear"; *Literary Matters:* "Punta Marina"; *Margie:* "Corpus Christi"; *New Ohio Review:* "Old Snapshots"; *Notre Dame Review:* "Beginning," "Fall," "In the King's Arms," and "One-Liner" (as "The Line"); *Ploughshares:* "Manhattan"; *Poetry London:* "Birthday in Middle Age" and "Side Issue"; *Salmagundi:* "Research Assistant"; *The Sewanee Review:* "Stragglers"; *Southern Humanities Review:* "The Protestant Cemetery"; *Stand:* "Consumption," "Legacy," "The Little Black Boy," and "Waking to the *Enigma Variations*"; *Stone Canoe:* "Dyeing," "Higher Criticism," and "My Computer Reads Me a Poem."

"The Garden," "A New Lover," and "Witness" first appeared in the Bright Hill Press anthology *Like Light: 25 Years of Poetry & Prose.*

"Wear" received a Pushcart Prize and was reprinted in *Pushcart Prize* XXXV. "Stragglers" appeared as *Poetry Daily*'s featured poem, September 16, 2016.

"Cain's Gift" and "In Hiding," originally published in *The Long Fault*, and "Death's Sympathy," originally from *The Art of Gravity*, appear here among the New Poems as part of the *Side Issue* sequence.

All other reprinted poems appear with others from the collections in which they were published. Rather than their order of publication, I have arranged those collections in chronological sequence according to the initial composition of most of their poems, though each book underwent considerable revision before publication.

I owe thanks to the Corporation of Yaddo for residencies during which several of the new poems first saw light or found their final shape, and to Skidmore College's Faculty Development Committee for funding travel that inspired a number of them.

My thanks to Karren Alenier and the Word Works for publishing *The Cutoff* as winner of the Washington Prize, and to Andrew Hudgins for selecting *How We Came to Stand on That Shore* for the River City Poetry Series. I am deeply grateful to MaryKatherine Callaway, John Easterly, and Louisiana State University Press for giving most of my work a good home. I also must thank friends and colleagues too numerous to mention here, and especially Penny Jolly, my muse.

LOVING in TRUTH

From *How We Came to Stand on That Shore*
(2003)

SELTZER

In a glass between my hands I hold the past:
not trickling through a choked transparent neck
but a deeper bubbling up
like used breath: clear, stony, bitter. All things

come back: seltzer—in polystyrene liters
whose screw-caps spray crazily round the kitchen,
a clear descent from the magisterial
blue-glass siphon that advertised *Good Health,*

presiding on my grandparents' tablecloth
squat, serene, mysterious as Buddha.
Weekly my hands would blacken with rubbing
Dick Tracy's pointy jaw in the comics

of the exotic Sunday *News,* as Zaydee
would stub his Camel out, slick back his hair
with yellow fingers, and produce the bottle
of yellower pineapple syrup. He'd pour

an unbearably slow dollop
into a tumbler sculpted like shul windows,
which I'd hold to the gleaming spout. I'd squeeze
the siphon's trigger—*khhhhh!*—and transfigure

the rainy day by effervescence so
the old light arriving through thickening
slabs of kitchen window, stuttering
through dust-scented lace curtains, would never

fade to dark. The seltzer-bubbles prickle
my nostrils like my pineapple schpritz's,
gushed from the siphon, its bottled power
threatening to burst: the charge of the Czar's

horses' hooves beneath the Russian sun springing
off swords, the trundling of bundles miles
and miles to port. Then huddled in steerage,
my grandmother creeping out, four, seasick,

begging the captain's scraps for her mother,
who ten years later locked in fury the door
against my grandfather, poor, apprenticed
to a tailor, affecting tailor's black.

One day when her mother had gone to market
he took those slender fingers in his callused ones.
They look out through the yet-unwavering glass
at a continent to conquer, a shining sky

(New Lots Avenue, where boys in payis
and black fur-felt hats belt a stickball,
their ears alert to the stubborn thunder
of the el's cattle-cars overhead),

and they stare together at the siphon
with all its bottled trouble, on the table
standing blue and solid as all time.
My grandfather shoots a jet into a tumbler.

He sips, gulps, and hands the glass to her.
All of fifteen, he asks her hand in marriage.
She stares, all of fourteen, into the glass,
sips, swallows, and turns to present her face to him.

VISIONS of GREAT-GRANDMOTHER

Grandmother kept the photo of her mother
on her nightstand until the day she died,
as if it could dictate what she should do.

Sometimes it did. Unflappable, fox-nervy,
my four-foot-ten grandmother, who once shamed
three giant muggers into running off,

recoiled into a childish helplessness
before the picture in its tarnished frame
weighty with silver fruit. "Mom, she's dead

ten years," my father would explode. "Do what
you want!" Yet who would dare to disobey
the face resplendent above that high starched collar,

the eyes gray and clear, excavating secrets?
Her nimbus of hair hid a mind like lightning;
her mouth exacting as the wide horizon

brought heaven to the full earth lip to lip.
I imagine Minsk as Byzantine, gold
mosaic domes, and spires, and minarets.

Fingers twangling on their balalaikas,
the goyim whistle folksongs in the streets,
needling my great-grandmother as she sings

a keen countermelody. In the cold
darkening house from her silver ladle
soup steams. Tonight we all can eat till full.

Across from me my grandmother's eyes glimmer
nocturnally, four years old. Out the window
shadows crawl as great-grandmother breaks bread.

Under her Nefertiti wrappings
and ritual corsets dormant fires flicker.
My grandmother's eyes widen. So do mine.

Since dawn I've had my woolens bundled with
my Chumash. Now we scrub each dish. Who knows
if we'll discover clean where we are headed?

The boat will have an orchestra, and marble
decks, and ices carved into ten-story
skyscrapers, and seven of every clean

animal. We will follow her anywhere,
even sailing West, West across the sea
to America, where the sun goes every night.

WELCOME to the FAMILY

When my mother's zayda died
the Brooklyn gravediggers
struck. The corpse lay ready,
the planks and pegs

of his plain pine box
required rot, so my uncles
shed dark suitcoats, hefted mattocks,
grappled among graves with shovels

and built a hole. The men
wore hats and their beards shook
fruitless sweat into the ground.
They knew they had to work:

time and law demanded it.
My father, the youngest, wore
his new suit
he'd saved for for almost a year.

Earth stuck and crusted it. The sun
dampened them all, made their
flesh heavy, redolent, rotten,
the hottest August on the books. My mother

not yet round but cousins buzzed
like workers round the queen.
Her skin flamed, her eyes glazed,
she woke up in the limousine,

her sister holding a compress
to her head. Till six feet
my father shoveled. He faced a face
of dark earth and felt made of sweat

and the cool ground, crawling with vermin,
delighted him. He stood out of
the sun, at rest, his blue suit brown,
then labored up ladder out of

the grave to make a pallbearer
lurching under the coffin, shaking,
making it disappear.
After dragging earth out, kicking

it back in was a blessing. Cool
grass grew next year on the grave
when the living met to unveil
his stone. I made the rabbi laugh:

gurgling and babbling, I puked
on my father's new suit, but I can't remember.
My goggle-eyes couldn't focus
the carved Hebrew letters of my name.

DID the BLACK-AND-WHITE MOVIES MAKE MY MOTHER?

Did the black-and-white movies make my mother
paint her nails black and nix all dates except
guys with cars? Yes! Joan Crawford forced her
to pluck her brows to crescent moons, and
Veronica Lake dragged mother's tress across
one speculative brown eye. Careening through Canarsie
in a Packard or DeSoto, her cheeks hollow,
drawing a Pall Mall's shooting star, she'd glow
at her 4F's futile strategies,
and my grandmother, snoring with worry,
would ascend from her dreams at 4 AM,
flustering in gerbil English at
my yawning mother.

                      Life became a process shot,
the real stuff rolling up front while the rest
receded furiously behind, where she ditched
the family candy store, having fobbed
her shift off on my wallflower aunt, promising
introductions, to snuggle down in the dark,
eyes glazed at duckboards in Normandy.
Where was the damn feature?

                      When the War ended
her serious work began. All those returning GI's! Where
was Mr. Blandings? My father, crisp and slender
in his uniform, a Jewish Sinatra,
was the first unhooked Marine she met.
Three years his long green limbs had leapt
at all instructions: how pliable they were,
how correspondent to command!

Some scheme!—as black and white as her
apartment thirty years later, gleaming
like a Warners or MGM publicity still—
Bacall, Lamarr, or Ingrid Bergman—a ghost
caught in the corner of a color snapshot.

MY MOTHER'S STUDIO APARTMENT

White as God, nothing wood, all glass,
mirrors and chrome. My small mother moves
about adjusting blinds and hanging prints.
Her best friend died three years ago while
Mom was last repainting. The funeral
took place in a mausoleum. The coffin
was jacked up and shoved in like a drawer
to molder behind a white marble wall.
Mom's stopped dating, entertaining, cooking.
She decorates and redecorates: "Our Pixie's
happy in her modern art museum,"
my sister says. Well, accepting. Looking,
she insists, for a smaller studio,
demanding less of her, moving
into smaller and smaller boxes.

THE PLANES CAME HOME
to the AIRPORT

Saturday mornings I padded about,
drank some juice, padded about
some more. What went *on* in there?

Later, at last, Dad would come out.
Dad would appear! We'd drive out near
the airport, and park by the highway
below the giant orange Erector Set
lights of the landing runway.

Then came the planes! They shook the air.
Wind slapped my face. Propellers growled
in envy as the new jets howled.
What kept them up there?
The turboprops, handsome and redcomb-tailed,
whistled for joy.
Dad hoisted me up to the sky,
where they came in so big and bullet-nosed
that I could wave to the pilots.
Once one waved back! before he eased
the plane straight down the runway bed.

I asked, "Do lots of people fly,
up there?" "Yes, of course," Dad said.

Daddy flew. He went away a lot.
I never woke damp from dreams
of burning runways. I never thought
those people in the planes
were coming anywhere but home.

HOW WE CAME to STAND on THAT SHORE

How we came to stand on that shore
I don't know, but in the failing
light whose diamonds
sank in the sea, my father threw
his arm around me and walked me down
the beach. "This place was gorgeous then,"
he said, waving his free arm at
the shuttered mansions and concession
stands. "I loved your mother, then."
Tar and glass cluttered the beach.
A steaming smokestack stuck
in the ocean like a lipsticked
cigarette in a coffee cup.

                              Why
we came to walk on that shore I
don't know except
for him to say, as before, "You
are the best thing I have done."
He'd stopped and stood stopping me.
"I've never told you this." The light
had nearly gone. Waves crept in
like sharkfins, dark against dark.
"When your mother and I vacationed
here, I know that there is where
you got started." I followed
his finger up to the boarded-up
window in the now burned-out hotel.

GOOD NIGHT

Every night Dad brought me to the casement
and I'd say goodnight to the Empire State Building,
radiant in its raiment and enfolding
me in its watchful spotlights, vigilant
as an angel. "Goodnight. Goodnight, Building." Pliant
in Daddy's grip, my torn, eyeless bear dangling,
I'd curl up, the Empire's steeple guarding
the watchful father and the sleeping infant.

I dream of him, his home by the sea, black
waves attacking and retreating. My back-
yard stream chuckles in summer, boils in winter.
In winter, surf sounds pound his bedroom window;
he wakes to no light falling on his ocean.
I dream this while my stream rushes on.

FROM "FIRST HAND"

> This my mean task
> Would be as heavy to me as odious, but
> The mistress which I serve quickens what's dead
> And makes my labors pleasures.

FIRST HAND

From asphalt to dirt road to muck
we drove up to her parents' place
that spring the One-Way Rental truck,
which settled outside the hand's house.
Her father helped in the downpour,
moving our student furniture.

He took an armchair in each hand.
"You'll make a farmer," he said, spat,
and hauled our sofa in. He grinned,
"And if you don't, then piss on it."
He came in again, soaked, and said
nothing, carrying our bed.

My head throbbed. My stomach went sour.
I grabbed the knob, searching for—
I flung open the crooked door,
but I could only see as far
as stinking cows munching cud
in the rain, knee-deep in mud.

Labor is neither blossoming nor dancing.
Labor is scrubbing, drying, sterilizing
the milkers, station, vacuum line, bulk tank,
shoveling sawdust, shoveling shit, throwing
thirty haybales down narrow chutes, clambering
over the bales in the loft, not even touching
a cow again till evening. Somewhere, watching,

her father's eyes see me in the loft, stumbling
on rafters and loose twine. He is all-seeing,
all-hearing: I know he knows I curse the stink,
the sawdust in my collar, the blisters rising
on hands too sensitive, long spoiled, now stinging.

Inside the empty, dark barn mind grows dark
and travels out the cleaner as it slams
the shit along. All I can do is sing
Sixties junk from the radio, or mutter
what poems I know and haven't yet forgot.
I'm caught in the barn's vacuum, in the middle
between unused-to work and useless babble,
developing my arms, decaying thought.
Her father, in for lunch, scrapes his platter
and slowly utters, in his barnyard slang,
a crystal from his tractor-thoughts, which gleams.
While I am laboring, he is at work.

Although we lie under one roof, my cloak
of sweat and animal odor, like her father's,
lies between us. True, I come in to smiling
eggs or chili patiently simmering,
which fortifies me in my fight, my one-
man trial of darkness. But after shoveling
the calf-pen's murky floor, or scraping off
the loaded milking platforms, I return
to her, painting and wallpapering for the wedding.
Crusted with the worst of earth, I find her
not keenly watching for bears and savages,

her knees propping a shotgun, but stitching,
singing, joining the scraps of her wedding dress.

SOLSTICE

The fat sun has stalled in the sky.
It stared me down as I awoke
and feeds on us while we throw hay

off the elevator. Break
can never come. The loft is never
full: though we haul bales and stack

bales all day, we can see the rafter
come no closer to our touch
but hang high overhead as heaven.

The bales keep rolling through the hatch:
we handle them as if they'd flame
beneath sun burning like a match

against our skin. We see steam
rise from us. The day stays, white
and perfect as a bad dream

from which we can't awake. Night
lives in another life, as bright
and far off as a wedding night.

ST. SWITHIN'S DAY

The seven cleanest cows crowd
the barn door, mooing, anxious
to get aboard. The sky is lead.
It's dawn or dusk. Her father wishes

silently, hard. In '42,
once it started, it didn't stop
till down town they had to row
the old folks out, pulling them up

out of their bedrooms into naked
air. Then they built concrete dikes
on the river. The hay got soaked
and rotted. Neither of us breaks

the quiet milking; we strive
mindful of Swithin's tomb, broken
to bring his bones under the new nave
centuries ago. The worshipers, shaken

and soaked forty days and nights,
watched their clay walls dissolve,
turned their boards into boats,
and saw the grave seal itself.

Now the cows don't low.
We offer work as hard prayer
to Swithin in the blackening sky
lowering on us like despair.

Although I have stolen his golden girl,
her father's features, softer and softer, smile
long, long into the night, until he blasts,
"Hey! Everybody listen!" The hardcore guests,
cousins, friends who've drunk too much to leave,
watch him raise his can of Stroh's, wave
a conductor's hand and tell the hushed chorus
the story of the Filipino whorehouse;
I've heard it half a dozen times in the barn;
but he stops short, just before the punchline,
and wanders into silence. No one cares.
Nieces and nephews practice swilling beers.
Drinking since morning, at last I get dizzy,
and keep drinking, listening to boozy
toasts, kissing cousins; then a strong arm gathers
my shoulders and turns out to be her father's.
Although I'm stopped, the living room still spins.
He talks, though I'm his only audience,
until, flattered and horrified, I see
the subject of his earthy joke is me.

THE ROCK and ROLL ANGEL
for B. D. Love

Who comes in clouds of makeup and flesh,
haloed in henna, lacquer, trash?
Who descends in garments like a star
and bursts new from the black hole of the bar
in a blinding aura? The angel
explodes in light and sound: fury estranges
us from his human form: his mascaraed
eye sears us all. The Telecaster
bumps his hip like a carved tablet.
Platinum strings gleam in their liquid
shrieking against the blood-red pickguard,
the melting voices of creation
radiating *Sin.*

Take us with you into the world of light!
Our world howls to us, but in your throat
is noise made music: it leaps off the frets'
dazzle and quickens in your larynx.
In the billowing fireball we merely singe;
your wings fan brightness, your silver nerves change
our blood to thrum with electricity
and rhythm engendered in the midnight city.
Thunder your unearthly progressions,
braid our frayed, diminished souls in sevenths,
and point! Animate these empty shrines,
our bodies, with your single Word: *Dance.*

STROWN BLISS, SCATTERING BRIGHT

Look at the lilac litter in the driveway.
You can't stop it; you can't help yourself
remembering its fragrance yesterday,
arching its purple handfuls above

the Dodge, leaking again. You glance from the petals
to my scalp, to the driveway's rainbow of oil,
and I watch you sadden at all this glitter;
you don't need to say it: *Why does it fail?*

Why does it leak away? You know. You know.
In your eyes I can already see autumn,
maples blazing, which like the lilacs lie
underfoot. But what carpets we walk upon!

THE VINTAGE

That Gevrey-Chambertin I stole
the year I worked the liquor store,
the year that we got married for
the rest of our lives sits still
in the rack, often the sole bottle,
the vintage we had planned to share
some snowy evening, when we'd stare
across the halo of a candle
years from now, reel back our movie
and laugh at candid photographs,
decades of diapers and grapefruit knives,
in a future ignorant of how we
burned our negatives to black
and left the bottle in the rack.

AWAKENING

My darling, snow arrived today and piled
up on the thinnest twigs, the lightest branches
like dust collecting on our candelabra,
more delicate—don't breathe!—than even your cold
dawn touch those Sunday mornings, before brunches,
the *Times* crossword, and football made us robe.

I don't know why I'm telling you all this,
trudging to the bagel shop alone
while you stretch out in someone else's bed
and wake him with your patented cold kiss.
I'm neither hoping that you telephone
nor praying that a climax knocks you dead,

just that you peek through his venetian blinds
while he's showering to wash you off,
and notice the snow's high-piled tracery,
white as sheets, that buries deep as romance
the branch in its unresurrected life
and tests the music of the chickadee.

A GHOST

I caught your ghost
   in an old snapshot where friends
      still drink and talk at our old house.
   It's winter: brown tweeds
      and blue sweaters hide every shirt and blouse,
and the window is blue-iced.

Still everyone smiles in my study,
   mouths open in mid-word;
      the only black-and-white
   corner of this old world
sits on my desk: the glossy
      8-by-10 portrait
   of your head.

Alone you stare out at me;
   our friends in color neglect
the camera.
   Your indirect direct
      pale gaze
   like a CGI effect
         next to a live actor
      throws
this world into an otherworldli-
      ness. Otherwise
         you're out of the picture.

The party whirls warmly about
   your face,
      which hovers
         in its own dimension,
   a place
      forbidden to lovers,
friends, anyone not
         paying you attention.

DRIVING in FOG

And now you're nothing and you're going nowhere.
Trees beckon you, struggling out of the vague
half-dawn and dissolving into the fog
behind you. The road emerges out of nowhere—
all ten yards of it—and runs straight nowhere,
the white lines stuttering, *No dream, just nothing.*
Wheel still feels firm in your hands, but your leg
has gone dead. What in hell are you doing here?

And now on the dim screen floats your lost
father, striding from a far land. Dim your brights.
Where's he gone? He sang that song you loved, you *heard*
it, *yes*. The same tree beckons. The same fencepost
flashes over and over, on each a blackbird
standing sentry in his red epaulets.

From *The Cutoff: A Sequence*
(1995)

IN the BOX

A baseball knows
its calculus,
knows
    its trajectory,
        each
        inch
            from the pitcher's hand,
    when it's scheduled to curve, or tail away
        from your downtown lunge
and leave you on your ass.
You can only guess:
    no matter how you study,
        how much you've learned,

a great slider or split-
    finger,
even when you see it—red dot
    spiraling,
white flicker—
        even when the *crack*
    starts everyone yelling,
        can devolve into a punk
            pop
            and flop
into the second baseman's mitt,
    or dribble you into a double killing.

In flight a baseball's an angel
    outshining sun or arc lights, its wings
invisible.
        Its blood-
        red
            stitches strut like seraphim;
            umpires alone have witnessed them,
                but at 90 MPH
                every stitch
                can catch
            the air some way an acoustician

   can understand—
and the ball
 sings.
   Hum,
  baby. Damned
if that ball
  don't sing. Music of the spheres. I've heard
it cauterize a hitter's soul.

Once Butch
 McCormack, down
  from the Show
   struck out in Omaha
 and tore the water cooler from the wall. When
we'd mopped the flood, he joined me on the bench.
"I've lost it. Lost the touch,"
 a man
  shut out from a mystery
 he'd once known and could never know again.
   Swings
  buckling the hollow of your knee,
    you howl,
   sprawling in dust, wrestling those wings
    invisible
  and always in the way.

AESTHETICS

Invisible in her dark lectures
   I'd see my prof's eyes
      shine like the blues
in saintly Venetian pictures,

but it wasn't Survey where I fell—
   she wore a Yankees cap,
      halter top,
and cargo shorts, playing softball,

a faculty-family pickup game.
   Crouching behind the plate,
      "Choke the bat,"
she told her son, on the other team,

who scrunched down lower at the plate,
   held the bat at the knob,
      swung at a lob,
and popped out into his mom's mitt.

When she sprang up I watched the long
   line from behind her knee
      up her thigh
(to study its sculpture with my tongue!),

and when she batted she poked
   a soft liner past first
      and burst
out laughing as she joked

with my English prof, who said, "Some
   mother *you* are." Quick laugh.
      Then she took off
on a deep double and came home.

You can't define it and not say "beauty":
    the pivot at second, the pitch
        that can catch
the breath like Keats, Klimt, or Stravinsky.

Yet I'd seen only hard-edge lines,
    a cool green right-angle world.
        A child,
I ran from fiery disciplines,

playing ball with a boy's passion;
    but seeing her on the field
        with her child
as mother, catcher, second baseman,

feeling a pang as she held hands
    with her husband, I saw
        felicity
in Passions of the Renaissance

as well as in a double play,
    in the curves of Samothrace
        or Koufax
or her exquisitely made thigh.

Three years in dark hush I hid:
    my heart thumped—she lectured—
        our transport
when she'd say, "God, that's a gorgeous slide."

SACRIFICE

It was like a Kamikaze
    mission, one out, three
        in, tying run on third,
on the bench we're wearing our rally
        caps, inside-
    out, looking like *re-*

tards, yelling our heads off, when Lamarr
    skies one
    to left, Skip sends Dwayne,
        the throw sails
        on the fly to the catcher but pulls
him six feet foul of home, the plate is clear,

and Dwayne decides to barrel
    into him and knock
him on his tail,
        he hangs
onto the ball,
        tags
    Dwayne out, and our jaws just unlock.

Dwayne regresses
    to fetal stage. His arms clutch
his knees,
    and he screams at the trainer's touch,
        so till the doctor
            arrives
we stand round him like Achilles
        and the Argives
        over Hector.

When Odysseus and his crew
    leave Circe's isle,
    human again but bound for hell,
they must yearn to ask him, "Why in the world did you *do*
that?" but don't dare to.
    We watch Dwayne roll
    around and want to ask, "Why in hell
    did you pull
    such a stunt? Why'd you bull
    into him and kill

the rally?" But we shut up.
    Dwayne's any of us. In his agony
    I see my years-long odyssey
        around the minors, a tour
        of battles and collisions, a Minotaur
    in Memphis, Medusa
in Phoenix, and the rapid
    dazzle
           of late sun on the scoreboard
        and off the women's seaside summer hair. . . .
        But hey, I would have scored.
I ain't *that* stupid.

EXTRA INNINGS

> The end of this game may never come.
> —ROGER ANGELL

Playing since two, I look up
    at the blackened
midsummer sky. Three up, three down, three up,

three— Top of the thirty-second
    as we head
for the all-time pro record—

"The hell we are!" yells Ed
    in center. "Fifty
if you play a pop into an inside-

the-park." Next guy, a lefty,
    wearily lofts one shallow, and before I can think
of rapacious obstetricians and my helpless baby,

instinct
    has me under it and I'm jogging
in, Ed calling me a blankety-blank.

As night cools down I hallucinate that winter's
    coming and we'll still be tied,
icicles hanging off the fielders'

caps, the diamond needing to be plowed
    every other inning, the game
spiraling on without end:

no one else can play either team
    ever again, my baby's born,
I can't help Adele, not there to choose a name,

I miss the high school graduation
    and the wedding and my first grandkid,
and I see myself falling down

dead
    diving for a liner in the top of the hundred
thousandth, spearing it to keep us tied.

THE SLIDE

Level
    as the field
    may be, from second to third, third
to home is all
uphill.
       Yet how often
          you must go *down*
       in the dirt and slide,
as if descent were arrival.

Ruth arriving fell
    into my astonished hands,
    having journeyed from her wetlands
uphill
    to my waiting finger-stones,

her head-
    first run through the nar-
        row channel, through the delta
        to safety,
a tough slide
    to the sea of open air.

You always want it to cease
    being tough, the channel
less treacherous
    but then you'd be heading downhill
anticipating the ax, your release.

Ruth's release into the relief
    of sweat tinged
        with air,
    air tanged
            with grass, had to hurt
            as this latest slide pained her aging father,
                late,
    tagged
            at the plate.
                Standing
after dusting it off,
                I felt the descending
        body, harangued
                by blood, relieved by dirt.

EVERYTHING but EVERYTHING

When Elizabeth at last accepts Darcy
   you've expected it so long
it's a surprise.
   You know everything
   except everything,
      as you know the copper beech
      will stretch
out in the sky but can't surmise
      each

gnarl, limb, or leaf.
   When I stand
out in left
      and we're far ahead,
   and Gary's got command
      of his slider, I see the game's grid
      laid
   over the ground,

over the green variables
of our skills
and lynx-alertness of our souls,
   how our beginning
      spins
   out of this three-out, nine-inning
      circumference
         we march into and then must wander
         through, the way a character
         in a romance doesn't know he's in a romance
         but takes ogres and dragons
as they come, as Dante sinks through circles
   believing
his goal's
      Beatrice
         while obedient to the thorned structure
      of the cosmos;

so the frame of the world depends
   on the horizontal dive at third,
      on Jack's leap in right, his glove just clear
of the fence
     to pluck the ball from air,
        and on the torque of wrist
that sends
         it sailing, each a local
         miracle
   without which this goodly structured
      frame would not exist.

We sail into the unknown, you and I—
   have we sailed too far?
      To navigate a marriage through the minors
        is like voyaging
into the old North Atlantic: Here There Bee
    Monsters,
        and we must guess
         the world is round, must suppose
    we'll keep striking shores
         where we can trade
         in gold
   and take on fresh water,
   and as far
as what befalls you and me,
we watch the coastline and assume we know
        everything but everything.

From *Venera*
(2014)

COURTSHIP at ISENHEIM

About love
   no one said anything.
      Raising his hand from under
  his wing
he raised her above
     all women. No wonder
       as she knelt
         in that heavy velvet gown,
           fallen hair flung down her shoulder, she felt
        let down

and turned her coloring cheek.
Her fluttering valves made her sneak
a look
    perfect for church
    had there been a church,
sly sabbath eyes nailing boys, not the book
       in her lap, where a virgin would conceive—
      who could believe
it?—a look
        she knew could kill.
        But an angel?

He was something, beautifully made.
Decked in gold brocade
   and red silks that swirled
      mysteriously around him, he kept his scepter
      back, kept her
at arm's length from his curled
      hair, his fingers
      articulate as a dancer's.
         In the red room
           a flint struck the steel chime
             of his bedchamber gaze
              igniting her desire to press
          his beestung lips to hers.

She would have died for that! but heard
   his sentence promise
     no angel,
        no man.
He gave his word.
            What could she say?
How could she seduce
    heaven?
               She felt her heart
palpitate, her blood
    hurtle
   as like a torch his eyes
   sought her averted face.
       Her free,
    unnatural
        Ecce
           hid in its art
           her nerves' unbearable thought:
    an only son
who would possess
    the only limbs to tangle
         with, the only heart to beat
    against her own.

THE KINDERGARTEN HEART

Kindergarten heart,
   oh Judy May,
how have the blue years hurt
    you? Memory makes the downy
       hollow of your upper
          lip lovely as any form rubble
         shot from the mallet of a sculptor
        has left in marble.

I moved away. All moved away
those years where Judy May
    and Lynn Soffer
       sit sipping milk, eyes
        lit, mischievous,
          their woodblock fortresses
   guarding the future
      where their sighs
         betray me
and offer
        love to men unworthy.

Their cascade of chatter can't hide
    the cynical curve
    of lip, the speculation of
      eyes that watch
the pudgy kid
    in drab olive,
       and bewitch
          him into a dream
   love
   will chrysalize and save
him, cracking to free him from the sad,
    balding, div-
         orced man he must become,

who sits in a room imagining
    their stares
at evening
        into their children's eyes
    and remembers
            when the kindergarten teacher
                Mrs. Silverman
        sat him in the corner after the kiss
    he still swears
            each awarded him when he handed each
                a handmade valentine.

ADIRONDACK SCENIC

The blue-hung clouds dangle, a wavering curtain
above the stage-flat lake, as though a show
were about to start—I have a good seat
on the cabin porch. An unseen cardinal
rehearses, some birds tune up, and from the trees
a wood thrush flutes an air like Debussy.
Offstage the loon begins an aria—
a *long* note—carrying it out onto the water.
A *long* note, a *long* note—and then it laughs,
it can't recall if this is tragedy
or *opera buffa*. Back and forth it shuttles,
deciding, and before I can call you out
to catch the ending of the second act,
asbestos clouds ring down, and I run
inside, battered with the applauding rain.

DAZZLE

For such blue this dazzle
   what sacrifice? None
  too great, none.
     Let liars in public trust go free?
     All day.
       Saints tear
       singer and soothsayer?
         Wives
          and husbands strop knives
  in the jealous sun?
       Out of our power. Our power
lies in dazzle,
   our responsibility

to such explosion
   as eyes' blue
   through
     my irising,
   through
       to the nerve,
         a perpetual
    losing
       of all
         but dazzle,
a flirtation
           with
           the perfumes of the palpable
     an embrace cruel as the grave,
        as strong as death,
          the sky in desire open
          upon
        the slow dazzle
    of this world, at once redeeming and reducing
us two
         in consummate dazzle
     to full
zero.

LIFE SENTENCE

At the bouquet of daffodils
from the prison greenhouse
    nurtured and gathered
        lovingly
    by the hands of a killer
        with Harley
tattoos,
hands that caress

the stems—as the guard
    marveling over his shoulder
    at his work has never
dared
        even in dream touch his wife—
            and then quickly coolly cut
        their green life
            out like a light
    like a lover

her look—
    sun burst from cloud,
    liquid
        fire you couldn't get
        even if you put
            all those blossoms in a blender—
somehow her look
took
        its light
        from the cut
flowers, a look
        that under-

stood
only the body
    in its volatile
        cells can create the nerve-
        shimmering wave
    we love to lie about and call
soul,
    love
    giving no reprieve
    no escape save

the daily
dalli-
    ance, the descent
        into the bouquet of fire where we give
        off
    all heat
    all light.

DIRTY LINEN

In your absence everything
    inhabits your scent:
empty coffee cup, sandwich, paper and ink,
    all redolent

as the nylon, rayon, cotton
    scattered when you unsheathe,
the pattern
        of their fall
            a deciduous riot,
        rhythms of smell
            rank as air sculpted by Sappho or Wyatt—
there's a man I really believe's in heaven,
        when her loose gown from her shoulders did fall—
    head spins to breathe.

Nerves flirt with overload
    till to inhale
one more charged
    molecule,
        one part more per mil-
        lion could kill—

Yet good is the life ending faithfully:
    to have all matter knock
with your olfactory
    hallucination, and public
    moments veiled with the pungent shock
of privacy.

ONLY CHILD

A small child is standing at the bed.
That's what you said,
    that's what you're saying as I shake
    off the shock
        of your voice
    rocking me awake;
        then your eyes

open
    and you chant this text:
        Can you remember what I said?
        Can you remember— —You said
        A small child is standing at the bed.
  —Before that, before I woke. I think I asked
Who are you? What's your name? Who are you? —And then?
—I can't remember what will happen
    next:

something
awful, something
    terrible.
        That's why I wake. —Something to the child?
      —I can't remember.
        Hold

me.
    You breathe deep, talk of your daughter
off at school, your boy
    off with his father.
        Imagine:
            the only child to get you up at night for water
    is the small child of this visitation—
        voice jingling
        like smashed glass, hand dangling
an eyeless bear—
            our child. I cradle you, your back
            and bottom sweating in the dark.
    We breathe together,
        and the dark at my back
cradles me.

LAUGHTER

> They resolved to invite to Florence the best craftsmen in Italy to make in competition, as a trial specimen of their work, a scene in bronze....
> For the subject, they chose Abraham sacrificing Isaac, considering that this would test the competitors in all the problems of their craft....
> —GIORGIO VASARI, *Lives of the Artists*

1

Anyone can model men from mud.
Make them better! Cast in bronze relief
to make us gasp and cast out disbelief—
in what? Is it incredible, a God
demanding child abuse? *infanticide?*
suffusing his concoction—flesh—with love
so faulty it flees at the drop of a knife,
its bronze clattering down the mountainside?
Well, *can you do it?* Entries must include
one ass, one fat ram anxious to dissolve
into a thicket, two slaves goofing off,
and popping like a rocket from a cloud
one punctual angel with a timeless shout,
zeroing on that bright glint at the throat.

2

Maybe any birth's miraculous
but if your husband wined and dined a stranger
billing himself as heaven's messenger
annunciating your new fruitfulness—
yes, you, enduring second menopause!—
so what if he ate with unearthly hunger,
turning your cakes and venison to ether,
your wine to air, your kid to sacrifice?
You'd laugh too. And such laughter! a music
ringing down centuries, preserved in books
like wedding roses, like a butterfly,
a dry, sly rustle snickering, a goy
in synagogue, the unbelieving smirk
of Ravenna churches, those shocked mosaics.

3
The angel gestures toward the ram. The son's
bound body torques up from the pyre, his eyes
nudging the angel's hand. The servants discuss
the happy ram, the donkey thoughtfully listens,
and a lizard, crawled from under the bronze
gleam of a stone, reflects. Even the father's
old cloak, flinging a threadbare corner, swears
that on a nearby cliff the ram sits and suns,
an obvious solution, overlooked
only by the old man, his forearm cocked,
knife mindless as a compass needle, his bent
body scything away from the quadruped
and toward the bleating boy, two souls prepared
for the bleak relief of disappointment.

4
And now the boy's become an animal.
Hear how he squeals! But you'd squeal too, arms bound
behind your back, your trussed joints swiftly browned
over the laughing flame heating the marble
altar to a shimmer. Your father's arms cradle
your dark head—inhaling, you almost swooned
beneath the caress of his hardened hand,
slithering awake as from a tonsil-
lectomy. Damn his passion for instructions!—
rigid as a falling campanile,
his stern robe descending in tiers. Your shrieks
fly to his ear, buzzing their sweet corrections.
He's deaf as bronze. Sometimes it takes an angel,
someone to grab an arm; whatever works.

5
Funny how it all happens in time's nick,
ticked on a fallen watch. We should have guessed
the kid's gizzard had to escape unsliced:
in a frieze on the altar hot as love's nook,
our superpatriarch redeems the tyke.
My hero, cries mama. Hands unclutch her breast
to take the erect bouquet. We are blessed,
and our grapevines hang weary with good luck.
Bronze seduces us to believe permanent
say, those absurd shoes that carried our first
steps, bookends for mother's family bible
through which our hero's boy lugs his bronzed moment
when, like cider laughing from an apple,
the spirit from his body could have burst.

6

How much richer, my life before the angel.
One time we hiked, and he knelt on the mountain;
I hadn't known a man might kill his son,
and I tried to laugh. Flames lapped like the spaniel
mother swore we couldn't afford. The tickle
of his bronze blade, excited in the sun,
stropped on my neck! If only he'd not seen
the ram. Years later, that rank smell of rough wool
made me weep for that knife, those wings, the tears
of joy my father misinterpreted.
Blindly I blessed my son, my heel, who thought
he'd snookered me. Ha! Selling soup to Stupid!
Soup! So light, dark, it all boils down to bless,
curse. What angel ever dealt with that?

7
The story ends happily. All survive
save the ignorant ram, white as a Hindu's
widow, scratching himself, oblivious.
The servants stop in midgossip. They knife
thorns from soles, and wonder if the stream's safe
to drink. The lizard flicks his tongue and crawls
back under his rock. The angel hustles
home, bolting his door. How can people live?
The father brings the son home to the wife
and over mutton stew they share a laugh.
The old man, passing on his old belief,
dies leaving the son to confound his own
twin sons, hopelessly blessing the wrong one,
life bumbling on in comparative relief.

From "Venera"

THE READER

So many distractions!—the angels crooning
next door, the organ throbbing down the hall,
out on the Sheep Meadow where she likes to stroll
crowds demonstrating at the fountain, chiming
like crystal. She's tuned out the singing, the groaning
virginal, the shouting colors of the parade,
and the jeweled gravity of her brocade
hangs on her like air. What can she be reading?
She happens to turn, happens as she turns
the page an old hand chances to have written,
her index finger marking what must happen.
Lips parted—chanting or astonished—she
happens to read the one book whose one story
chances inevitably to be hers.

THE MOTHER

Not my mother, certainly, not any-
body's mother, yet despite the down-
cast glance, her face glows—that serene playground
look you see on young moms in the city:
engrossed in bestseller lust, but if some bully
tries to nail her lamb, her clear, alert skin
will hum brave as an apple, and struck blind
by love the little thug will slink away.
Such wide-set knees could magnetize a lover
marking beneath her gown a field of power.
Enthroned as on a birth chair, she delivers
us with one push into the universe,
rays of light loosed from her loose-shaken hair—
oh my, my children's, everybody's mother.

THE LIGHT

The gold light's created in the east trees,
abrupt against trunks, lovely in the limbs
looming like X-ray bones. In these rooms
new light makes everything antique—the brass
bed, oak dresser, last night's whisky—suffuses
the rediscovered world like gilt combs
combing gold hair, winnowing from my dreams
streaks of sheer light whose falling mess of rays
eliminates the need for clothes. White light
at day's height batters us from far above
the trees, wanting nothing to do with skin's
effusions or healthy glow, but like night
indifferent to the colors of my love,
the gold light that dances around her bones.

THE SISTER

In the Park marching, voices ringing, at stake
all vulnerable virtue, "No more!" they shout,
"No more martyred sisters! Take back the night!"
By day the tower rises and the lock-
smith labors. Some of the best will starve stuck
in penthouse keeps, some stumble in the street
where a knife at the throat cuts off debate.
Don't be oblivious. Put down that book.
And when the dance floor heats up, don't react;
keep cool, a phoenix—no smiles, no eye contact:
that de la Renta suit conceals a slasher.
"Hey, sister," whistles the construction worker.
"Is it a good book?" whispers the junk-bond broker.
How shall the world be saved, beloved sister?

THE FIELD

But into what shall we beat our plowshares?
The grain strains skyward with the best of us,
but my love keeps its vigil in the furrows
where zygotes sprout in passion, where the source
suckles the jailbreaking seed, drunk with tears,
until, against the air, it joins the lace
lining the field's lips, only to shoot like rice
back earthward, raining on us in the mire's
embrace. So all aspiration recycles.
Love straitens us to drag us in the ditch,
one of the universe's dirty jokes
you wouldn't tell at the drunkenest party.
But it's our joke, our love that's rude and dirty,
and when my lady suffers an itch, I scratch.

THE ARK

She's so well-built, so trim, that any wind blows
her gently. Despite the warped world, she weathers
the wickedness of pimps and undertakers,
steering by her constellated virtues
her living cargo through the roughest seas
to port, where she must fend off smirks of sailors
and smart remarks of salesmen; and she batters
them back simply by averting her gaze.
In the warm hold, hidden, the animals
smolder, steam wafting from their hides and nostrils,
spring coiling round them, long cooped up, kept chaste,
a rumbling as in the guts of the earth—
can she keep these beasts clean, mad with their fast,
this keen desire desiring to give birth?

THE HANDMAID

After traveling all day you'll arrive
half-dead, an inn where upstairs you'll discover
a bed so made you'd choose to sleep forever
or immortalize the shredding ache of love
as though such verging on climax were life.
You'll ask, "Who is the angel of this chamber?"
and hearing water poured into a laver
turn and be taken by her. How to save
her from these rooms, the dusty uniform
in which she curtsies now, how to transform
her—jewels! robes!—what words of veneration?
A kiss might lure her into bed, where you
might barter some cheap ring. Such dreams, my hero,
such velvet longings. Such imagination.

THE HOUSE

The house is packed, stacked. Bodies assemble
to watch a ballerina in a hush
of music—make it Suzanne Farrell—push
sex skyward into an ethereal
realm. Here in the fourth balcony hearts tremble
at such elevation, her arabesque
rippling up through the dark while ushers blush
at the elongate angle of her ankle.
The Gothic architecture of her body
obliterates all sense of ours, its lame
excuses melting with its aches. My lady
is built like that, propped up by knees and elbows;
the shelter of her hair, her hearth call, "Dance."
Enter, and be danced to another home.

THE EARTH

Deep in a black hole see my bluest lady,
blue luminosity fixed like a jewel,
tilt 23° from vertical
the axis of her head, her upper body
and mind bent like a divining rod toward me,
allowing me latitude from pole to pole.
I hope no more than to play her footstool;
the curtains of her robe descending round me
bring night lit by aromas of the sea,
the harbors of a sunken continent
of her desire rotating hourly by our
jeweled movement. Why turn to lighter day?
Stay to rain on this mutable planet
nocturnal seed, oh nacreous seafarer.

THE FOUNTAIN

All things flow from her. We know her tears
create the stinging sea, and when she sighs
the ferries founder and the porpoises
and whales can't focus on their own discourse
for the disturbance. These are the waters
of life, the bitter fluids fleeing her body's
perfection with such speed that when her piss
drills a road to the earth's center, all wars
suddenly cease and enemies tumble in.
Her flowings are the means by which we mourn
the dead, the living, and those never born,
for mystery is in her menstruation—
like manna her ministrations trickle
into wine I drink from a crystal bowl.

THE GARDEN

The trials of being human, the terrible
things they do out of passion, behead you, lock
you in a high tower, fire arrows, break
your quick legs on a wheel—all for the rabble!
In the garden the martyrs make their noble
march with the touching outrage of the meek,
waving their palm fronds high in the air. Look!
They want to be trees! That promises fruitful
salvation: not to die, but to feel birdsongs
trembling your privacy green as Daphne's
changes. Whoever heard such strange branchings?
Dressed in green desire still my darling climbs
skyward, still reads, still sings her arias,
lovebirds and lovers wreathing in her limbs.

THE SINGER

Or else her voice is such an instrument
as wrings grimaces from a singing angel,
a robin's wrangle, not a nightingale,
carrying a tune, otherwise untrained,
an instrument of evening, a voice blunt
as wet leaves, the rotting odors of fall
and mourning, yet with such a strong fertile
call as makes rutting spring feel imminent.
Via those obstacles to melody—
her teeth, her tongue, her barely opened lips,
her mystic media conducting my strange
trek inside her voice—her notes, like Möbius strips,
bring forth themselves, each naked flowering tree
shedding fragrance over and over like song.

THE BRIDE

Chasing my darling through the snow-lit trees
to a room in a realm where rain always rained,
I knelt outside, spying love through the blind
and fingering the pane, its cracked glass
splitting my view between dress and undress,
light breaking from skin emerging ungowned,
unblue, unvelveted, my sight unstained
save for that other between her and my eyes.
Imagine my shock, my severest charge
short-circuiting broad waking dreams of marriage
with wet lips full of syllables that spill
like flung neon through rain calling *Motel,*
a sign, like light cast out of her forehead,
how willingly she could be spirited.

THE MIRROR

If marriage as a mirror of our world
gives us the ardent pair, blood-red bedclothes
funkily fragrant, garden-lit windows,
wood clogs, a little terrier, what world
does *she* reflect? What message does the gold
leaf back of her translucent skin disclose?
Speculation spreads like a cellist's knees;
she's like no other, mirroring each mere word
she reads, so what she reflects is mystery.
I ache for her to apprehend me, perfected
in her jewels' white light stupid as a star,
or to swing her eyes suddenly up at me—
I'd enter their reflection, her deep mirror.
That's the world to live in, all in her head.

THE TABLE

The angel is in love with her. He wants
to break his contract as the messenger.
He wants to speak for himself. But what terror
in choosing the dreck of human romance,
to feel wing-feathers scatter to the winds;
worse, to have to eat, to kneel at her altar,
he who's never so much as tasted water,
his airy gorge rising at those communions:
the bread not even bread but always tasting
like human flesh, the wine rich, disgusting
as blood. Yet he'd eat at her board, he'd grow
bones for her; if he could encounter her by
chance somewhere, a garden say, even he
might offer her some food, some fruit or something.

THE LOVER

Love lies, neither emotion nor disease
but a text the flesh hungers to decode,
demanding a translation into blood
and gilt. See how the book of everything lies
upon her lap, as open as her face
whose downcast eyes have passions to confide
to the page, turmoils that, objectified,
would straiten me if locked in her embrace.
Lift your luxurious eyes off that page.
Nothing there can save us from the ravage
of the skin's quick touch into bones—old themes
crumbling our entwined bodies downward grace-
lessly. What remains!—absorbed by your face
absorbed in your reading of these poems.

From *The Art of Gravity*
(2011)

INVOCATION

Apollo! Onstage I stood
in leotard
and slippers, white tunic knotted
    at my shoulder, and I *knew,*
        like lecturing on quantum mechanics
        or batting, bases full, against Koufax,
    here I was, in trouble again. Apollo!

Oh dreams, fraught
    with inadequacy—
can't I impersonate
    a god in the privacy
        of my unconscious,
        dance
under cover of tactful night
        in a dark house,
            with no fear
            of a true mirror?
        Elusive muse!
    Then at my elbow Mr. B

(ten years dead)
materialized. I said,
    "I've never danced—"
        (at *all,* I meant)—
            My dear,
        he interrupted, his accent
            purring in my ear,
                you
are god
    of muses. You see danced
            ballet
            how many times? You know.

Thus bemused,
thus blessed,
    I (who'd never
        danced), I was Apollo,
            set for the strains
    of Stravinsky's score
    to course like ichor
           through my veins.
The curtain rose; I woke in the darkest
        hour and never knew
               what immortal long-legged darling he
                (in conspiracy
with night) had cast:
            my Terpsichore.

MUSEUM

Quick sidelong glances
    clodhoppers in fourth position
        and you know
    this young woman
          you're trying to conceal you're studying studying
    with you this Degas
dancer dances
    so it's difficult not to imagine
        as you watch those flinging
        painted limbs the flinging

in precise abandon of these legs growing
    out of her clunky
        shoes like saplings springing
        from the pavement and inclining
          their two trunks
    like lovers toward each other irrevocably
        seeking a crux
and disappearing
          into the short
          shade of her black skirt.
          Art

is exciting. As you peek
    from the paint to the paint
        on her eyelids an identical
    mauve under Degas's light
and this, she shoots a look
    too quick to be meaningful
    and you've stopped breathing right
        so you haul
your attention back to the work
of art from the work

of art. Yes.
Yes the forms. This
    should be a decent
        enough interval but when you look she's gone
       so you turn
    to see her walking, turned out
    out
         into the next gallery.
       Hurrying to the center of the room you yearn
to raise
    your hand *ah despair* but that
        seems silly

so from afar you watch her thick-soled slenderness assume
    second position in front of—
        does it matter? The dance
        must go on, her exit, your entrance
this absurd chasing from room to room
        of art that must insist on inspiring
    you and give
        you nothing, nothing! you! savoring
           this fruit-
           less pursuit.

LATIN CLASS

Herschel will be pissed
I know. We missed
last week and have practiced
    exactly once even
    after I cobbled some Van
    Dyke Parks and Steely Dan
        into a fake merengue tape.
        In a panic I tell you it's hope-
less but your Presbyterian genes insist
            so we try to look invisible
        among the couples trip-
            ping over each other in the high school
            gym and shrug when Herschel's cool
            skeptical
    eye stares us down.
He seizes Christy his partner by the wrist
        and they whip
            around each other in an impossible
    new step
    hips driving like some insane
    Caribbean machine
        and the others' jaws drop
            yeah right so I can tell we're all on an equal
                Anglo footing. We walk it through
            fast way too
        fast he cues the tape
        and suddenly it's carnival
    for spastics screaming out for correction
            Fellas! Fellas! oh
the wrist
        this way the hip
        that and now I'm not step-
            ping on your feet and the planetary whirl
    and shift of weight and tension
        in our arms feel

>   fine
>   as I catch
>   you in the orbital
>   swing and watch
>   your eyes light up Caribbean
>   while Herschel
>   bails out of our lurch-
>   ing path his smile
>   I imagine
> barely suppressed
>   at us the Dominican champion
>   *estrellas orientales* as we dip
> dangerously only to rise up in the East.

SERENADE

When they waddle into the pizzerias
or the cafés, craving sun-dried tomatoes
and artichoke hearts, you realize they're kids,
babies, whom not so long ago their mothers
swaddled up and shipped off to the city,
gambling the farm on an absurd dream
that ducklings become swans and girls turn dancers.
And here stand seventeen upon the stage,
knockouts made up like nobody's business,
an abstract of blue gowns, their untamed hair
still lush, yet unimprisoned in a chignon,
and look: no longer girls but goddesses,
no longer children wearing baseball caps
and hanging out in restaurants and bars,
lipsticking their ludicrous cigarettes
and rattling like immaculate dice ice cubes
melting like fortune, like an audience.
Now, raising right arms in a gesture of
desire and protest, *Noli me tangere*,
not until they suddenly shift their feet
in unison on a Tschaikovsky chord
do we swear we'd barter our souls or kill
to know the touch of the untouchable,
because those arches, pointed toes, and spaces
glimmering between limbs initiate
a transformation from the merely human
into illusions, into symbols not quite
approachable, not quite warm-blooded—into
dancers. You must know the wonderful story
of Balanchine inventing *Serenade*,
how he made every section for the number
of dancers who showed up at class that day—
he was working with kids, after all, kids
knowing nothing of time, being as gods.
Their puberty and immortality
depended on that first step, that conferral
of divinity by a man who knew,

sometimes, the terrible seductiveness
of restraint, a genius who adored
their teenaged tendons, their thoroughbred limbs,
who understood to set them to Tschaikovsky
would be to set them in the Pantheon.
And when they descend, when they issue through
the stage door, wearing baseball caps no team
has ever worn, and tee shirts of such samite,
so baggy that we study all the harder
the stainless muscles of those sacred arms,
we *want* to feed them, having read of nightmares,
the starving and disgorging, we feel protective
as of a lover waking from the depths,
we need to scent the sacredness of art
because they wreak wild havoc on our glands,
infecting our blood, infiltrating dreams,
plaguing with romantic imbecility
an otherwise sane, fleshly congregation.
No wonder we relax, though startled, to see
them munching on ambrosia, sipping nectar,
seltzer rather, ordering a pizza.

SCENERY

Nature bores me so
   it's a relief to find out
      the Romantic landscape
         with its irradiated
            round trees or haystacks, its deep barred shadows,
  and its clouds galloping across the sunset
      is a painted
   backdrop,
         and the boisterous
         verdure of the lush
  shrub lit
  not
  by sunset but
            by sun
  a painted flat
         one
    dancer uses to prop
     herself up,
            and that the flowers
can bestow
            odors

only of tulle
   and sweat and, faintly, dyes,
  paints, or appliqués,
     since those swatches
of lilies
     and mums dancing against the painted sunlit bushes
     are, yes, ballet skirts, their hems and stiff stitches
the most unnatural
     thing in the world. I love to watch as
       art
     triumphs, as first one dancer in the wings snatches
         up her shoulder
         strap, then another

  and another, their hair the preposterous
    red of matches,
their rapid steps burning the natural
       air
until
  with a tempestuous
       crescendo in the clear weather
       it's over
    and smoothing her floral skirt
  the prima ballerina curtsies
    and clutches
  the brilliant bouquet, flowers
    smacking of dreams, betokening lust, luscious
and unreal.

REHEARSAL IN SUMMER
for Kyra Nichols

The *oddness* of attending a rehearsal:
the starts, stops, half-steps, the wobbles off pointe,
the ballet master's abrupt clap to signal
the lagging pianist—it's not yet art,

as though you, all along, were reading rough
drafts of this poem, its grammar wobbly, rhymes
askew, and meter pirouetting off.
But through the stage's mottled chaos gleams

the luminosity of bodies at work:
the prima ballerina's bucktoothed smile,
even in cruel daylight, without make-
up to soften her stark, big-nosed, beguil-

ing homeliness, makes the outdoor stage light up,
then dazzle as this long-legged thoroughbred
bursts into a horselaugh at her missed step.
She hitches up her baggy neon sweat-

pants whose faux clumsiness can't disguise
the brilliant rapidity of her limbs.
Her strange patience when her callow cavalier's
not getting it: they try a few more times

that tricky spin where he must catch her at
the last conceivable moment, then they try
again, and yet again in the beastly heat
until finally they look heavenly

in their saturated practice clothes.
But now she stops the pas de deux: the tempo
keeps getting stuck, it's like trying to dance
in mud, or on a stage marleyed with flypaper—

a plunk; a stumble; and now the pianist
at last nails the Tschaikovsky. All at once
the crazyquilt colors of practice clothes
collude kaleidoscopically, the dance

obliterates mere muscle, heavy lifting
translates to flight, and sublime locker room
aromas float off the dancers, wafting
our way to settle on us like perfume.

ADAGIO

Slowing, the oboe swoons in the orchestral
swell: if a girl denoting six o'clock,
thrusting one leg behind her toward the sky
were not enough to make us gasp, that leg
imparts momentum to her head's downstroke
so her forehead touches her other knee,
all this on pointe—enough to make you fall
in love a hundred-fifty feet away.
I loved a dancer once, and watching her
do that with her body in front of two
thousand people I suddenly couldn't breathe
until she'd lift her head once more and lower
that leg I knew, and send me on toward death—
that firm, amazing leg, those years ago.

EXUBERANCE
for Sigrid Nunez

Drunk of course, so we were dancing up
the proverbial storm in our hosts' living room,
cutting a Persian rug. I caught you in my arm
and swung you round one, then the other hip;
then, back to back, I launched you in a flip
overhead. You kicked their Tiffany museum
piece, the chandelier. In the tomblike hush—our tomb—
it swung wildly, slowing to a heart-stopped stop.
Nights passed like that in our exuberance,
lit from within with a bright stupid grace
that wouldn't last—our high-stepping destroying
other fixtures, stained shards glittering
like jewels. Barefoot, reeling on smashed glass,
no wonder we overthrew the bloody dance.

MID-AIR

A dance that ends in mid-air doesn't end.
The stage blacks out, but there's no curtain call,
for even if the curtain should descend

the dancers, turned to shadows, still extend
their breathless steps behind the fabric wall.
The dance that ends in mid-air cannot end

for Orpheus, bound for a distant land
bearing his torch into the lightless hall,
where even if the curtain should descend,

eye losing eye, hand suddenly seeking hand,
the glancing blow of tragedy won't stall
the dance that ends mid-air: it cannot end

all gravity, the dancers' upright friend
who sets them leaping, keeping us in thrall.
Then even if the curtain should descend

on our performance, looking back we send
our bodies forward, leaping to a fall—
a dance that ends mid-air and doesn't end,
not even when the curtain must descend.

THE LESSON of ORPHEUS

You play blind. She depends
   on you, her dead legs
trailing in your dance.
You advance
      by echolocation,
          chords plucked from gut-strings
      like light raptured from the sun
   into the gloom. She drags
   you down
   one step for every two you rise, and tugs
       at your shoulders where she clings
   like exquisite stone
     wings.
     She longs

to twine
around you like a vine
   to crawl
all the long way up from underground.
     She demands you see her,
        embrace her flesh bruised like fruit,
         claim the clammy papyrus of the winding sheet,
      the hiss in your ear,
    the keen perfume in your nostril.
     Sheathed in the sound armor
     of your lyre
        you ravel out music
        to trick
your veneration
    into desire.

Who has not tried to revive
a dead love?
   Dance floors,
      dinners spiked with wine

    and regret, hours
        silent, supine,
            uncoiled on sofas, hand
            chilling in hand.
            The papers all but signed,
            we went out dancing, a kind
            of celebration. My hand

massaged the muscles of her back,
    those twin embankments either side
        of the forgetful river,
its undulating current a swift shock.
    A sigh, the dead
    weight of her head
        on my shoulder:
I could get her back.
Flick:
        my eyes opened: I made her
        disappear.

Navigating her through Hades'
    lips back into life,
    braille hand reading her chest for breath,
        her nipples
for a word, heart stiffened for stillbirth,
you dance close
to the surface,
        rumpling the crust like moles,
            near-
            ly breathing air,
faint music through the humus,
    a lilt in the loam, the beautiful filth
        you'll never scour out from under
    her nails.
    A bird warbles

                diminished scales,
                        her joints' percussion
                    knocking nearer
                        and you turn, you always turn
        to see her iris
                        spiral shut, the dawn
                    fold its petals
                        into stone.

TRANSLATED

Crowned
    with an ass's head you get to partner
        the queen, the queen
        of fairies, the queen
        of the company. Stumbling as in a swoon,
            as if you've lost your glasses,
    you're bewildered how this creature
            with her ethereal
                limbs and unimaginable
            crevices
extends to you beyond
        the reach of vision
    her gossamer
        softnesses
        veiling your eyes
        ludicrous with happiness.

Yet you partner beautifully,
    your braying and tentative trotting
somehow supporting her in the pas de deux,
    responding
        to moonlit promise,
    handling
her sleek calf and royal thigh.
      It's everything
          I dream of, someone
            to scratch
    my ears and admire their hairs sprouting
        and in devotion
      tender my wise
          age
        parted lips, open
    limbs. Open eyes.

DANCE of the SNOWFLAKES

I have never paid the weather
enough mind never
    taken the year's turnings
    as intimations or longings
        of any but my own and not some human
        global or cosmic condition

so it's time to dance
attendance
    on the snow not the snow
        we shove out
    of the driveway and the plow
        plows back in not
the creaking shushing snow breaking the liquid silence
        beneath my skis but

the breathtaking white body
    we can apprehend
        if we care to its crystal
        glint and shimmer its structural
        miracle
    its ability to suspend
our intellectual pertinacity

so the revelation *it's snowing*
    descends with accumulations
    of flutes and violins
        in an insistent
            swirl
            a circular
        flurry whose silent
concealing
    uncovers an elegant
        structure
    this white body tempting the hands

because the snow as it piles up acquires
    density and heft

      though that's not what I'm after here
      rather
the illusion that, falling, it's soft
that it's living and passionate that it coheres
that as it snugs and embraces this world we imagine ours
it cares

about us the way we fantasize
    those dancers
flurrying onstage to Tschaikovsky's
        music care, skittering, gliding
            singly
                then collectively
snow flying from the flies
            no sign
    of the storm stopping
a squall of tutus
    a body of dancers
a corps of course, the ballet's
            crystalline
intricacies

visible from heaven
    the fourth ring
without magnification
how the tulle and satin
and flesh of the human
women
        whose implicit joy and desire now burst mysteriously
    into song
        collect in a mathematically
    intricate and moving

corporeal
    mass,
    aromas
        arising from their sweating and scented
    bodies

    to travel
        I imagine heavenward

yet each one on pointe unique
    in the construction of her hands
    in the instructions of her genes
unique unique
        in her eyes and lips
            in her fingernails
        her steps
            following those of everyone else
unique

as each snow-
    flake
        beyond its six-
        pointed generics
           on pointe
and each toe-
        shoe a point
    points engendering an oblique
        angle its vertex
            a fine place to start
            isn't it
        a vortex
            a good end
                a human shelter
                from weather
    this genetic
                flurry
        these emerging imagined
white limbs of snow
                embracing, enfolding, each one different
                melting me.

MAKING a FOOL of MYSELF
over MARIA KOWROSKI

Streamlined as the ornament on a Packard,
swan in takeoff under the ghostly blue stage
light, her face a sphinxlike, impassive icon
    chocked with Tschaikovsky,

she's a dancer Balanchine would have loved, loved
bone and sinew, heir to the muse's mantle,
lunar-cruel and stupid with genius: music,
    movement, and blank sex

knocking not the crotch but my chest and poor brain.
Charming? More like paralyzed: eyes gone flashbulbs,
air turned flame and raptured from lungs, my glib tongue
    dumbing to granite.

Later, wrecked, I'm meeting her face to face, her
twenty-two exquisitely unabashed years
smiling through some party our town has thrown these
    dancerly creatures,

cheese, champagne, some boxes of Girl Scout cookies.
Glass in hand, "Maria Kowroski?" I say,
"You—your dancing—*thrilling*'s the only word. I
    sit in the dark, thrilled."

Smiling, she is cooing, "How sweet!" but no—it's
hell, not sweet—I want her to know I'm kept up
nights to partner succubus limbs that burn the
    phosphorus air, so

quick they torch the dreck out of human passion,
moonlit arms abandoning me to darkness.
Now her smile is faltering, now my wife says,
    "Don't be afraid, he

gets this way sometimes, but he's harmless, really."
God, I've bought a pair of your satin toe shoes,
battered, hardened, stripped of their ribbons, nude pink,
    ragged with pointework,

shoes your feet have danced in, where sweat-conducted
contacts sparked to generate light, divine toes
crammed in boxes signed by your hand. My hands now
    fondling your footsteps,

hear me out, Terpsichore, on my kneebones:
drive me crazy, cripple my days with beauty;
naked relics clutched to my cheek, I breathe their
    reek of sheer ether.

SONNAMBULA
for Darci Kistler

What a party! brocaded ladies,
their bodices flirtatious
    as armor,
        the air exploding
            in sequins and thick
as narcissus
    liquor—
            what
slender promise
            for the poet!
morose,
        romantic,
      believing

in nothing
    not even it seems
        poetry—
            when down
            from a garret, a tower, down
        among the jeweled finery
        down
    from dreams
      wearing nearly
nothing,
        a nightgown,
        a shift, down
    from asylum
        she lights, candle-laden
among the living.

No breath
    stirs her flame
        that even the wind can't extinguish,
    yet it is flame,
        it would singe,
it would translate helpless to do otherwise a moth
    to ash.
        If you turned
            her gently
            by her visionary
        hand,
            she'd spin on pointe endlessly
        almost. If you twined
            in her limbs and pressed
            against
        her nightgowned
        body
            if this could be a body
    and not an apparition,
        a ghost,
if this were no dream—

The hazard
    of this occupation,
        this precarious
            craft! In the teeth
        of the evidence
I'd
    commit to her, this nightgown,
        this slip, this sylph
            in her unnatural
        strength
        worth . . .
            well,
    to dance like that! like no one!

I'd
be carried
            by her
    effortless-
            ly up her tower
up over the jeweled
gaping crowd,
                the poet
committed,
            a glimmer in the air,
            a flicker
                in the night:
        farewell.

From "Danses Macabres"

DEATH GOES to a PARTY

Death does the hokey pokey and he turns
himself around. Music makes you believe
hair grows on scalpless skulls and bare bones jive:
look at those party-animal skeletons,
piles of knuckles, pothooks, and plumbers' joints
reveling naked. They've got to grin, they wave
to a corpse tumbling in an open grave
with worms bopping about its sunshine bones.
Thus concludes the history of the world,
no whimpering but a great rowdy shout,
a clatter and crash like crockery, pots hurled
about the kitchen, hipbones shaking it
in and out, all bones set on making it
one last smashing time. That's what it's all about.

DEATH'S COMFORT

It comforts me Death's flat-out impotence
can never stimulate the limp to rise—
tempting and cold, level as wilderness,
unleavened as wafer-bread. Who wants
dead darlings to suffer resurrections?
Elbow grease could not stop Lazarus
from stinking, nor desire help Orpheus
from flinging Eurydice a backward glance.
All art aims to flesh out how we reject
the dead. Yet here Death stands, flush as gangrene
with lust, his skin dripping in putrefaction.
He has designs on her, he'll dance erect
behind her and seal her purification
with his John Hancock on her ghost-white skin.

SWEET DECORUM
for Sarah Webster Goodwin

One fiery breath and down like dominoes
they tumble. Death's triumph, the Great War: ranks
of boys rising like zombies from the trench
to dance in No Man's Land. Machine guns hose
them, spattering the earth so little grows
despite the plowing underground by tanks,
despite lifeblood and fertilizer. In France
white crosses bloom for miles. Demure in rows,
scrubbed as schoolchildren in uniform lines,
like girls not yet menstruating, unkissed
they lie. We lie to say they lie asleep,
a sweet nap after a sapping field trip,
as if they'll wake to milk and macaroons,
their carved names saving them from getting lost.

MATTER of DEATH

Ambrosia, angel food cake, that's how sweet
Death's excrement should logically tang,
victoriously hurled out with no sting,
maybe a tingle tart as pomegranate
seeds, clitoral, resilient, radiant light
escaping. We rescue jewels from dirt, loving
the way anatomy attracts the tongue
to honey, plunging the nose in the pit.
Once Dante wriggled blindly up Hell's sphincter,
buggering the final mineshaft, that center
of Gravity. He rhymed—after his exit—
its brilliant voidings: the heavenly starlit
dome. Light can't hold a candle to dark matter,
which outweighs all we see. Death's shit is shit.

HOROSCOPE
for Joseph Caldwell

Go out dancing and you may break your neck.
Show others your keen and morbid sense of humor.
Highfalutin theories sound great, but rumor
has it you will come down to earth. At work
enthusiasm will infect you. Check
your physical woes and your health at the door:
family could be impressed by a tumor.
Purchase a plot of real estate for luck.
Mention what you want, and you won't get it.
Paranormal abilities may surface.
Reward children with praise and legacies.
Let love stab you in the back. Start a riot.
Confuse the issues. Lose hope. Be concise.
Stop all this nonsense. Lie down and be quiet.

DEATH MAKES the MAN

Cue lightning to flash, cue thunder to pound
against the cellar window while he stitches
some last embroidery. Now he attaches
the electrodes—but before the resurrection
he stands back to admire his manly hand-
iwork: the polished bolts, the zillion switches
that flip the nervous system, the jeweled crotch's
artful setting. Yes, topnotch skin and bone,
quality parts, for he recalls his younger
cock-ups, that Hollywood job that still lumbers
flatfooted like a hippo through his nightmares.
He needs a dreamboat, not a Schwarzenegger,
something to lure the young girls from their chambers
for dirty dancing, a member that remembers.

DEATH the DIETICIAN

She won't eat, she can't eat, but that's OK,
she must impersonate a rail to dance,
she must maintain her cold line in performance.
Potato chip or two, try to choke
a cup of yogurt down, a Diet Coke
say, every other day. He calms the parents:
it's good to see them dancing in their bones,
the scrawniest, the unripe—those he'll pluck.
He's got this thing, see, less for little girls
than women slamming the brakes on being women.
He gets off on the flat chest, on the prison
of a stark ribcage, on the annihilation
of the bloody cycle. It's no curse,
fruitlessness. That apple he munches was hers.

DEATH'S THEATER

It's not all tragedy; he's not averse
to melodrama if everyone gets shot,
or musical comedy if the plot
is big and earthy, with a crop of chorus
girls good enough to eat. He loves a farce,
that nervous frenzy, those doors slamming shut
in your face. He's Mr. Opening Night,
top hat and cape, arriving in a hearse,
knocking them dead, each show a limited run:
one performance, curtain up, curtain down.
He'll undertake conning supporting roles,
rebuild the sets, rewrite your lines. He peddles
tickets, and pens reviews in which you shine.
He sends flowers. He coughs through your big scene.

DEATH'S ADDICTION

Death inspires you and fingers every stop,
tickling your holes with whistling breath, his hot
wind playing your bones like an Aeolian lute.
And in his embouchure's embrace, at his lip
like a cigarette, you inspire him: each deep
drag sucking forth your soul can illuminate
nothing but itself, a red warning light
filtering you to ash, down to the tip
of his finger. You are his cancer, you fill
his lungs with the luminous holes he thrives
on, and drawing you out he scans the bar
for the next sucker who desperately craves
his cure. Grinding your butt under his heel
he lights one up and takes her to the floor.

DEATH'S ANIMATION

Shot out of an inkwell in the Fleischer
Studios, Death tapdanced in jazz cartoons
fronting a corps of corpses, skeletons
and Betty Boop—a *ree*-al hoochie-coocher,
sweet Betty, rolling cow eyes as her jitter-
bugging garters sparked like séance hands,
inspiring ghosts to ectoplasmic dance,
knocking joints into an upright posture,
a future cocked of animated bones.
Filmgoers flipped at headless resurrections—
such a gas that *hi-de-hi-de-hi-de-hi*
a star was born, *boop-boop-be-doop*. Far away
in Europe ink fled back to the black bottle
for soon bones wouldn't dance, or rise at all.

DEATH SINGS LIEDER
for Tom Denny

He's a poet, Death's a goddamn poet,
Romantic but nobody's fool, a tear-
jerking good read, sucker of sap, extruder
of juice. The young maid fears she's going to get it.
Oh where, oh where's his heart? She sees right through it,
she screams *Don't do it,* she wails *Oy vey iz mir!*
Reading her fevered lips, he translates fear
into *Darling,* crooned in Ultraviolet.
Singing her delicate and beautiful,
Death gets under her skin, where he'll tease out
what shines in her. His hand will stroke, not slap:
he'll make her purr, not prey, tame as any cat.
By the time he rings his final rhyme, she'll sleep
soundlessly, head hard on his clavicle.

LA VALSE

Only Death can keep commitments: girls flirt
and withdraw, flirt and withdraw, the music
consumptive, languishing as lust grows sick
and dies. Wallflowers! One fluffs and smooths her skirt,
and with her white-gloved hand she masks her heart,
then her face, until he sweeps in to take
her in his arms like an electric shock
while the waltz threatens to blow itself apart,
thundering, screaming. Dyeing her ballgown black,
he offers her a mirror where she can read
no reflection, the glass cracked and opaque.
She lets him gather her, waltzing, and freed
from time, she's raised dead-center. Around
her race the idiot dancers, hand-in-hand.

LAST DANCE

Fifties sock hops mortified us, necros
in death-embraces, the teen dreck we listened
to morbid as puberty. When they found
you in his arms, my girl, America's
girl, high school ring clutched tightly in his knuckles,
its 7-Up bottle-glass emerald ground
to dust, your T-Bird's radio still moaned.
Your car's shards had divorced us, sure as sickles
cutting grain. We could never dance to it;
his last kiss would linger on blood-red lips
I never got to smear. Now, heavenly
shades swooning with your rapture, thunderclaps
for bass drums, it's number one with a bullet.
Darling, he sings, *save the last dance for me.*

DEATH'S LOVE

I saw an old man hobble down the street
on the arm of his grown grandson. It touched
me, those generations linked, his claw hooked
on that arm, that stride helping his shambling gait.
Then his eyes probed me from their sunken pit,
young, positive as new blue stars. That spooked
me, smooth skin stretched over the skull. I looked
at window dressing till they'd passed, then sat
sucking ice cubes chuckling in a tall drink.
Grow old along with me. Could I live marriage
in real time while mad acceleration
sped my darling toward light? Our skeleton
masks hide skeletons, so it's no joke
how Death loves us and molds us in his image.

DEATH in DISGUISE

By no means young, but she was not old either.
Like rain I recall the afternoon her songs
first swerved baldly off key. The clockwork springs
of my childhood went *ka-boing;* I cried. Mother
by the end wore her body like a sweater
shrunk comically too tight, like Death in paintings
with skin the tarpaulin color of tarred lungs,
a master of disguise dolled up as cancer,
the true comedian as the letter C:
twining himself round any alphabet
as subtly as snaking through a tree,
he steals away our speech, leaving us deaf,
dumb, screaming we must shuck love, regret
life. Comedian? More like the letter F.

DEATH the MOTHER

Stevens nailed it: Death is the mother of Beauty.
I know, since Beauty endlessly would bitch
about each bruise, about the jealous watch
her mother kept. Like twins they looked, uncanny
as mother-daughter douche commercials. Tasty
all tarted up, mom couldn't act her age,
embalmed in heavy scent, flaunting a bonus flash
of flesh, that black lipstick. Beauty would cry,
cursing her mom for teaching her the dance
that she, by nature, couldn't help but lead.
She brought me home, and it still thrills and sickens
me how her deep-voiced, long-legged mama, clad
in Beauty's lace bra, cocktail frock, black stockings,
lay in wait all night to jump my bones.

DEATH in the WOODS

My wavery window glass makes it appear
something out there's moving among the trees,
out where the woodchuck nibbles at the grass,
out where the raccoon feels that rabid whirr
like a lawnmower savage his nerves' core.
As I shift my weight behind the glass,
tree bends to tree, unhelped by any breeze.
I hear them whisper, and I know conspir-
acies green with chlorophyll are afoot:
he's sprouted leaves for manufacturing
his own dark sustenance; his parasite root
nurses at the breast of my decomposing
mother, and his blossoms broadcast spring
to hide the preparation of his fruit.

RECEPTION

What had that wedding dress to do with white?
For you were something borrowed, something blue,
shrouded in eyelet, white skin shining through
like moth-holes in a lampshade, and I dreamt
how later that night you would radiate
a love-glow like a bug-light's indigo,
as luminous as chemotherapy.
Who'd guess you'd planned to disappear? As night
dropped its veil I surprised you in the barn
grinding your hips against one of the ushers
I didn't recognize, an old friend of yours.
The bone-web of his hand kneaded your luscious
buttocks, sawdust soaked up your bridal stain;
you pressed lips on teeth, dancing flesh to bone.

BREATHLESS
for Hilary Sio

I dreamed I brought you back from underground
and for a time in time I repossessed
your breathless self, whom gravely I undressed.
Your stocking's black whisper under my hand,
your black garter's stutter against blood-drained,
squid-white flesh, the ultimate minimalist
art, despite your time passed away, amazed
me with arousal. We danced again, we sinned
as if there were no tomorrow. Each tear
that sprang abrupt and human to your eyes
sparkled and said I dreamed. You weren't there
after all these damned years: ever faithless,
the party girl, sucker for a black leather
jacket, ever the dirty adulteress.

DEATH at MIDNIGHT

We knew it would be touch and go. My songs
proved fruitless. They caressed you in the cradle
but you left anyway. At night I still
hear distant dancing music, the plucked strings,
the clucking of the bones: on flapping wings
he drops in to adopt you, kiss you, snuggle
you, then climb dark air as on a bicycle
while night wind rushing through his bone-spokes sings.
My babe so beautiful! it chills my heart
with terror just to look upon your stone.
I see you dancing naked in some Death-
run nightcare center, a blueblood spoiled from birth,
instead of planted in the pristine dirt
where you have not and never can be grown.

CURTAIN CALL

The ballet master tendered his gaunt hand
and made you immortal. I'd never seen
your eyes so dark, skin so pale, legs so open
to choreography; your suave new friend,
not I, would partner those fine bones in the end.
Phantasmal, Pavlova dancing the dawn,
rising elusive as a dying swan,
your steps echoing in a distant land,
for years you dazzled him; his company
grew desolate without you. As you dance
away, I'm left with smoke and intermissions.
Linger among us longer than customary
for a last curtsy, *la grande révérence*,
clutching fall flowers before blood-red curtains.

ENVOY: COME AWAY, DEATH

Now, at last, I've grown sick and tired of Death,
his filthy lust, his holocausts, his craving
for martyr-bombs and subway gas, his dancing
in vile denial like a psychopath,
his upbraiding my loved ones in the earth.
Grief's time-consuming and hardly beats living.
I won't dance. That stopped when I watched my darling
strike her last attitude, bereft of breath.
The pen she left me just dropped to the floor,
staining our red rug black with ink. A car
door slams, late-year Mercedes, triple-black.
Who's got my shoes? A hammering at the door.
Bang goes my alarm clock. Time to stop work.

From *The Long Fault*
(2008)

TEMPERA

Explosions bloomed everywhere after
the autumn fireball, the skyscraper
unzipping. Forsythia flamed
through the neighbors' fence and consumed
the pickets. This morning, the egg
I dropped stared sullenly back,
its primordial tempera
smashed to raw glue on the ground,
the yolk that could feed and fix the world,
that medium for Gentile's
and Simone's miracles,
the Magi with their camels, Mary
who with just an egg made history.

SUBLIMATED

Fog rising from fallen snow
overleaps the liquid state.
That's how I would like to die,
raptured from gross solidity,
a subject saved from predicate
the way a single contrail splits
in seven in the barely blue
of barely air: the shuttle crew,
evading intervening states.

We aim so high because we're low,
citizens of gravity
collating wreckage that can't soothe
lovers at the grave. Low
flags mark our sublimity
while higher reaches thrum our nerves
as if, in the flaring scratch
of a phosphorus-perfumed match,
some human element survives.

BOOK BURNING

Fire loves paper
but adores people.
Fire eats our words,
hurling them off
like flaming birds
on bright black wings.
Smoke must cough
but fire sings,
breathing deeper,
sucking down
our oxygen.
Fire is not
our brother's keeper.
It isn't a question
of good and evil;
it guzzles the broth,
consumes the table.
Heine guessed
a modern truth:
they burn books first.

The night of the fire
on Unter den Linden
what rang up the curtain
next door at the Staatsoper?
Die Zauberflöte,
its gorgeous noise
lit with love,
a book of seduction,
light, and learning;
we walk through flame,
daring hell and high water,
dancing and burning,
our fancy fired up
till real tears drop.
Or *Tristan und Isolde,*
romantic hell

on a Celtic ship,
love mating death
till both look the same;
fire crests the wave
of the blood-dark ocean,
extinguished breath
blood-wet with kisses:
lovers, poison,
and none left to blame.

On the Opernplatz
the students wave
a sea of dark arms
engaged by armbands
and oozing the spume
of cream-pale hands
awash in the air.
Goebbels commends
their courage to break
the intellectual
reich of the Jew
and homosexual
and face the blaze,
courage to erect
in this vast empty platz,
banal and funereal,
a tower of books
and feed them to fire
like so many faggots.
The boys pledge death
divinest respect
with courage to burn,
courage to burn
Freud and all joy,
such men as Mann,
heretic Einstein,
and Heine the Jew.

The opera disgorges
its lovers, their eyes
still moist, songs still
in their teeth. They view
the night turned day,
the spring turned hell
this early May night.
The spines crack.
The burning covers
issue a smell
like living leather,
rank with authors.
Kerchiefs mask noses
and hands shield eyes
raised to the skies.

Another decade
and they'll take burning
to the very Beginning,
the primal Word,
spinning the world
back down the commode,
back into its Chaos
of mud and scheiss.
For now, bringing brightness,
words of all people
soar in a tower,
the babble of languages
melting together,
the fire-breathing steeple
drunk on air
and publishing ash,
singing like mad
a single song
in a single tongue.

ASPIRATIONS

But really, it's enough to make you gasp,
this gambling, this dicing with the world
order as in a game of Risk,
calm, murderous words like the rasp
of a bastard on a marble obelisk,
filing history to sand, polishing it bald
as a missile whose aspiration
to join the company of saints in heaven

comes crashing on the neighborhood of Eden.
We always want to think we're something more.
The woman longs to be a god, the man
to be in love. The serpent's subtler,
rehearsing to be master of all matter.
We dream we all own souls, sucked in like air,
and that aspirates huffing along the palate
and fricatives tickling the teeth are spirit.

As I lay on the operating table
naked under the childish laundered gown,
awaiting the needle's sucking of my fluid,
I rose to an unpinioned aspiration:
to keep intact my bundle of meat and blood
for touching, scribbling, loving, nothing an angel
could fall for, no inhuman appetite
for slaughter under cover of bearing light.

FOLDING the FLAG

With a lover or friend
stretch it out waist-height
and parallel to the ground.
Fold lengthwise so blue midnight

with its strict constellation
vanishes under pure white
and blood red, a frisson
along the stripes, shot

between you. Fold again
lengthwise, a lot like unmaking
a bed in which no one
is ever just sleeping.

The stars should stay outside
as in the universe.
From the stripy end, fold
it up in small triangles,

kissing when you meet.
Tuck in the end, creating
a cocked newspaper hat
from whole cloth, a thing

useful in comforting
a suddenly public wife
suddenly veiled, her gold ring
shining like eternal life,

like moist eyes, like the bright stars
in her jaunty souvenir cap,
the weight of their universe
pressing into her lap.

THE GUY WHO PASSED ME DOING
90 MPH and PLAYING the TRUMPET
for David H. Porter

Left hand in charge of steering, his right on his
valves, lips compressed—jeez, how could his embouchure
hold firm in thruway traffic?—why this
lunatic didn't create fresh carnage

beats me; the speeding jerks on their yammering
cell phones lead sainted lives by comparison.
I love that blessed solitude while
driving, that heavenly, insulated

half-hour or so so quiet except for my
car wheels revolving, turning the world under-
foot. Cool and modern, hot, baroque, or
classical? Armstrong or Miles or Purcell?

So What? or Copland's *Fanfare*? Or *Taps* for those
cut down like grain as Gabriel harvests his
highway? Yes, *Taps* for everybody
jamming the planet, those half a dozen

more hornmen blowing up the proverbial
storm, burning ancient charts in a riff like an
X-ray whose tonic revelation
rouses the dead to the flame of sunrise.

LOOKING OUT

I open the box of shades, these glossy leaves drained
of life, to guide
    your photo up, my monochrome
        Eurydice.
From your white windowframe
you study this living room,
        a teenaged scientist,
      evidence swirling before you
      condensing into a new
        cosmos. In the past
you wonder at this bald head,
          the phenomenon
           of color,
            and just what power
has plucked you from your underworld.
              Love
    doesn't occur to you.
        The future
            rides on your adolescent armor:
    your serious yet almost
        smirking stare,
    the silly ribbon
        struggling in your hair.
  Silvery emblem,
              uniquely positive
        document of your teen-
  aged face, hardly
  art, hardly
            life—
  ghost with a gleam,
shade
        in your fifteenth year,

                        forgive
            my averting my
                        gaze in favor of
                  your fleshly heir
and lowering you once more to your dark bed,
                  your chaste
      dream
                              of the fulfilled life
            you cannot know
                  you haven't missed.

NETHER STOWEY

Dear Coleridge, I'm a stranger in your house
and do not think of you as lunatic
or some nut nodding off to opium,
but a man feeling too keenly the touch
of other human beings, who needed air,
cold air around him to anesthetize
his overloaded senses just enough
to get on with the grim business of living.
I'm shivering to be breathing in your parlor,
this small room where, sitting in colloquy
with birds singing bower songs, leaves blazing, ice
lengthening in the winter moonlight, you
all conspired to bless your son, sleeping,
inexplicable as a foreign land,
love offering the principle of translation.
The sad past melts away in the sublime
cold. Dorothy tells how you walked the knife-edge
of Helvellyn—on either side a sheer
drop—at night, in shoes with licorice soles.
In childlessness I hear your pen enact
those words—*My babe so beautiful*—scratching
the midnight silence like a record groove's
promise of Mozart. The missing film
that fluttered on your fire I've loaded in
my camera, the little chamber I use
to violate your intimacy. Make me
a companionable form. As much
a stranger as on barging in, I steal
away hearing your strange nocturnal words
collect, turning my head sadder, stranger still.

JANE AUSTEN, INVENTOR of BASEBALL

> ... it was not very wonderful that Catherine, who had by nature nothing heroic about her, should prefer cricket, base ball, riding on horseback, and running about the country at the age of fourteen, to books....
> —*Northanger Abbey*

How to learn the signs, how to decide
to commit, how to know mere manners from
true ardor, how to take a pitch, how
to hang in, how to foul off Wickham's trick
deliveries, how to connect with Darcy's
devastating curve or Mr. Knightley's
high hard one, how to dust yourself off from
a brushback, how to parse the rules to your
advantage, how to plot a strategy,
how to work out the crucial late walk under
fading light with the moon rising over
the fence and nightingales singing their anthem,
how to protect your lead, how to hit
and run, how to rally when visitors
keep chipping away, how to play defense,
how to guard against the steal, when to play
for one and when to try for two, when
to sacrifice, how to negotiate
long-term contracts, how to determine if
and when it's safe to come home, how to read.

ABSORPTION

Stare at a color till you become the color
and red fields with fiery barriers surround you.
Painting absorbs you, and your world grows fuller.

The canvas reaches out to you. Get closer,
drink from deep reservoirs designed to drown you:
stare down that color, dare become that color

clutching you, turning your eyesight duller.
Faint green ghosts wrangling in the red confound you,
the paint absorbing you, your world grown fuller,

flusher, the canvas raving like a lover
whose words knock in your head. Without a sound you
stare at a color till you become the color.

Now take these late blues, deep blacks, and discover
your cheek not dark but drained. Put it down to
painting absorbing your life, growing fuller

of every shade, abandoning you to pallor
yet reaching from an absence so profound you
stare at its color till you become—no color.
Paintings absorb you, and their life grows fuller.

IN CAMERA

Eternal life via a hinged wood box,
   a silvered plate, a man drunk
   on the stink
      of visionary chemicals:
         pneumonia, scarlet fever, a rheumatic
heart, anything plucks
        off a child of nine, leaving a thick
           Victorian glaze
         on its eyes,
     a bruise where its skull's
          been passionately kissed,
           a body perfectly composed
        for worship on the settee, no nervous tic
or blink
       to blur the work
           of the daguerreotypist
aiming forever to fix
           nature
           here in the parlor.

Light's remains absorb us. Whatever reflects
   can illuminate
     the silver buried
deep in a dark box,
   sun banging on metal, a sleight
     to gong the spirit
back to our world, where artifacts
       (this corpse's dazzling image, ferried
        to new life in the palm)
          can, after full immersion
         in poison,
       thrive in a wood frame,
     a cold child offered
on a cold, reflective plate.

From your frame
   on the piano
     you smile, Father,
  as if you didn't know
       a grimmer image knocks
       in my mind's dark box—
    a grayer picture,
   your face grisaille as old snow
into which your headlong frame,
      like a filthy joke,
    a pratfall at a formal dinner,
       lurched prone
          and made a last impression.
    Neither gin nor
       formaldehyde, not even
       the polished, hand-joined oak
coffin's casement window
    from which you cast your
       frozen last look,
      could put the trick
        across, the bright illusion
you were at rest, or warm.

THE GOLDEN CHAMBER

They found the girls buried
outside Cologne, creating
a sensation. Before long
strange stories spread.
Of course they were girls
no longer but skulls and sticks,
flesh, gowns, and curls
long dust by 1106.
A slipped pen in translation
confirmed St. Ursula
and her eleven thousand
sister virgin martyrs
breasted the Rhine in eleven ships
to be slaughtered by
poleaxe, sword, crossbow,
faint smiles and the kiss
of Christ upon their lips.
Eleven thousand virgins
yield a lot of bones;
the newfound martyr lode
(though many bones were men's)
boomed the relic trade
yet piled up many a cartload
to stock St. Ursula's shrine.

How do you articulate
the bones of eleven
thousand skeletons?
A scapula can't recite
whose shoulder fleshed it once;
even skulls with jaws
keep silent intercourse.
A mystic had a vision
of virgins by the dozen,
each floating from the mist
to offer up her name,
but none published a claim
for her kneecap, rib, or wrist.

The head's a reliquary
for the skull, the skull
for the brain. Artisans
carved elegant wooden
reliquary busts
to snug the unfleshed
crania: young women
born of the cut live tree,
modeled on the living
daughters of Cologne,
their delicate wood hair
curling like the Rhine
framing painted faces
we might mistake for angels',
betraying subtle smiles
as if a virgin's innocence
housed the hoariest knowing,
the way the softest skin
provides a smooth disguise
for understanding bone.
On the Feast Day of St. Ursula,
October 21st,
the daughters of Cologne
would each take up a bust
to carry around the church
and out through all the town,
hundreds of murdered virgins
miraculously reborn,
the same golden dresses
and wise, shy smiles,
the same gold tresses,
the same violent Rhine.

And the wooden girls return
to their ornate gold niches
in the Golden Chamber
where today their smiles burn
a hole in the heart like a small

death. The upper
walls of the gold room glitter
with rustic herringbone stick
patterns as on Adirondack
great camp friezes.
Then the illumination:
they're bones, thousands of bones
horizontal, upright,
slanted, stacked, piled,
sorted by shape and size,
tibia, fibula, rib,
the bones of hundreds of virgins
raised to ornament
this gilt and gruesome bower,
a grand memento mori,
a golden charnel house
bequeathing us a foretaste,
bones blissfully composed,
articulate at last,
chanting a cappella,
spelling VRSVLA.

MENNONITES by the SEA

Those nearly naked sauntering by, breasts
bikinied and buttocks thonged, rolling along
beneath white dazzle, before the turquoise sea,
their moist, sun-venomed fascination—vanished.
More than the dolphin leaping fifty yards
from shore, a group of women has swept me
off to the elemental realm of Homer:
not Nausicaa and pals tossing their beach ball,
but something homelier, the world of Winslow,
at once boldly and shyly American.
Mist rises from the sea around these barefoot
six in their brown, black, slate blue, wholesome gray
ankle-length frocks, sedately bobbling, pigeons
among the jungle flock, their tresses tucked
in tight white muslin caps with strings dangling
in the sole gesture of devil-may-care.
The youngest of them runs along the beach,
hair unbonneted, bunched in a white scrunchie.
She teases her bearded father in his homespun
trousers and suspenders, his boots redeeming
him from the burning sand, his broad-brimmed hat
staving off the classical sun. The sea
kisses the women's hems, infusing their
skirts with its brackish solution. They enter
a step, a step further, the ocean spanking
their dresses against their limbs, unexposed
and pale, until the fabric snaps like spandex
on a hip-hop siren, or Nefertiti's
splashy wrappings. How deep will they wade in?
They wear their dresses as the fish wear water,
as if no one were watching, no one lying
nearly naked and nearly unashamed.

A BREAKDOWN
A. R. Ammons, 1926–2001

Coming from anywhere, your poems, they traveled
anywhere, rucksack on the back, hitching
up dungarees, hitching a ride, sentencing
down the road, letting their hair down, letting
themselves tumble down scroll-like and pushing
their lines through all those colons, never flinching
from all the nonsense we push through our colons,
compost being our biodegradable
identity, giving away the game,
giving off heady perfumes, signaling
hey, all the crap we spin out of ourselves:
haute cuisine for someone else, a fly, say, or
bacteria, imagination just
another enzyme, how the whole damned process
of breaking down never breaks down, whoa, never
ends, only that in the localest terms
we end, ending up brokedown into spelling
and if we're lucky intimations of
some glory and some end that we use to
distract us from that glory and that end.

THE COLLAPSE

The snow ganged up in March
on the roof and around the walls
of our summer cabin,
an old ramshackle Sears
catalog design.
It proved the finishing touch,

for while it was wombed in snow
the cabin could enjoy
something it never dared dream:
structural integrity,
red walls like an ancient tomb
stowed in a white barrow.

The field mice scurried and pissed
and gnawed toothpaste and soap.
The mute typewriter sat stiff
and composed; come thaw its type
would rust. The upright, tone-deaf,
froze out Gershwin and Liszt.

Late in its term, the snow
in the sun's lengthening flame
relaxed its crystal flesh,
tormenting the cabin's frame.
The roof knelt in the slush;
the modular walls fought free,

a leisurely explosion
we found Memorial Day.
The floor entertained the roof;
the six-foot sections lay
spreadeagled on the earth,
none of the windows broken.

SUCH STUFF
Charles LeDray, Tower

A high stool perches on a Rietveld chair.
The Rietveld sits upon a Shaker table,
the table straddles
the ridge of a little house
that rests upon a chest
of drawers supported by
another chair, another table, on down to
the stepladder, the sideboard, the great sprawling desk,
and the wheelbarrow leaned against
an antique bedstead stood
on its head—the world piled up on this precarious
three-foot tower the sculptor
carved, the label says,

from human bone.

How could anything human take
in hand a just-cold human rib,
put its mortal architecture to the knife,
and whittle into virtual
life a ghost-chair from this scrap of perfect spiral
that guarded a heart?

Is everything material?

One man's mate had been his bone,
such stuff, still-
warm, fashioned into flesh,
black hair and an insatiable
instinct for fruit and information.

Thanks be to knowledge, the canker,
the drop of vinegar we might not notice
corrupting the wine. Thanks to the curator,
we know our medium,
the assembly of our clean, cruel furniture
into the strange
balance that maintains us staring
speechless on this brittle, beautiful tower.

CARMELITE CONVENT, MEXICO DF

Past portraits of sedate saints
at desks like grade school principals,
past dormitory cells where nuns
once whispered prayers to iron bells,
then sank to wooden biers and slept,
we descended to the crypt.

This death-intoxicated land
gives skeletons the final chuckle.
They play in a mariachi band,
hack a laptop, dance flamenco,
sing a feather boa torchsong,
soar on batwings, fish, go drinking—

Death makes mirth in Mexico.
The jawbones slacken in a laugh,
the lively, eyeless sockets know
nothing ends in an epitaph,
for pleasure lies in getting stripped
of everything. Then, in the crypt,

the glass-topped coffins let us view
the corpses of some denizens
of a colonial century,
some of abbots, some of nuns,
others sporting finer dress,
all whitened by the same distress.

A person often mummifies
in the capital's sapless climate.
Though ancient gum sealed one nun's eyes,
some woolen and some fleshly habit
had worn away. Thus she gave us
a peekaboo flash of naked pelvis.

Others suffered harder wear,
ribs poking out between the buttons,
their boots, sewn of the supplest leather
for bourgeois metatarsal bones,
each now clumsily damned to dangle
from the slenderest, whitest ankle.

We couldn't say they lay at rest
because the mummied mouths stood open
with this or that peculiar twist
as if their maiden glimpse of heaven
contradicted what they'd heard.
Every body looked appalled

on death—or the death of an illusion—
though one skull, maybe once a lawyer,
grinned with clean white satisfaction
atop his once-tight, boiled wool collar
grown ample, the kid glove on his fist
skinned back to bare a knuckled wrist.

MEMORIAL CHAPEL

We've arrived expressly to be transported
while we sit stock-still in the college chapel's
1800 Federal architecture,
    witnessing music,

Schubert, Bach, Prokofiev, Shostakovich,
week in, week out, making this room a spare, sparse
paradise, a garden where sound waves loiter
    rounded to crystal.

Now, for instance, Beethoven's Grosse Fuge in
B-flat major scrolls from the quartet's guts while
listening I study again the names carved
    back of the players,

marble-clad memorial to the Great War
dead, the undergrads and alumni who got
butchered giving Europe democracy it
    didn't desire and

lie transported off overseas. The Grosse
Fuge spreads thick, deciduous layers, aural
flavors—ash, ambrosia—in living ears un-
    stopped with the earth, un-

like the ears of Wesley D. Karker, Luther
Hagar, William W. Waiteskill, Herbert
Rankin, Talbot Carmichael, Allen Ashton,
    Kennedy Conklin,

Wolcott Caulkins, Alwyn G. Levy, Howard Thorne, and
dozens more stone deaf to the music, deafer
than a post, than Beethoven, college guys now
    deafer than when they

sat in boring lectures and dreamt that bloody
high romance, imagined those French *jeunes filles,* but
found nothing transporting them, no returning
      even as cargo.

THE HILDESHEIM DOORS

And here I'm sitting on a low stone bench,
but not a bench, I see now—it's a wall,
an old foundation round a grassy patch
whose center, a six-pointed memorial,

marks where the fringes brushed the parchment scrolls,
then blessed the lips, letting glad voices sing
the Flood, the flames of Sodom, chariot wheels
sunk in the sea, the fleshy reveling

around the Golden Calf. Half Hildesheim
got flattened by the Allies in '45,
plane following plane, bomb following holy bomb,
mere weeks before Red tanks inspired the love-

death in the bunker. In the marketplace
Hildesheim's good burghers schemed to rebuild,
timber by half-timber, in full Renaissance
variegated splendor, the butchers' guild,

a charming resurrection, and so clean
you'd expect the master butcher to be Mickey,
chauffeured by Goofy decked in lederhosen.
But it's for real, bearing out the lucky

destiny of a city that embraces
its own terrible role in history.
In the southern quarter a host of houses
survived the bombs, their sixteenth-century

frames jauntily crooked, plaster walls whitewashed
spanking clean. Just one building went to rubble,
this synagogue, burned down on Kristallnacht.
It's easier to make a memorial

of something that's no longer necessary.
At Hildesheim cathedral, great bronze doors
one thousand years old spin out the twinned story
of fall and redemption, of fruitful loss

and bloody victory. Their style shocks us.
It's frighteningly modern: Adam and Eve
fling spindly limbs over their nakedness
beneath the blasted prehistoric tree,

their fingers pointing everywhere to stain
anyone but themselves. They know. That serpent
curling among the flowers like a vine
has lost his voice and can't plead innocent.

Their round mouths wail in cartoon disbelief
at the rough justice of their sentence, numbered
from Day One. Moony heads smooth as if new-shaved,
plucked out for shunting down a ramp, they're tumbled

toward death—for stealing fruit! sun-ripe and warm;
we bear helpless witness. Smiling in wait,
wearing his dark suit like a uniform,
the sexton flips a switch. The lights black out

and brother kills brother under an eclipse
worthy of a crucifixion. No angel's
words to Mary, burning through space from lips
to virgin ear, can light these bronze rectangles

chock-full of God's love, each comic strip panel
a boxcar coupled on a one-way track
to terminal, screaming right on schedule,
rectangle after rectangle in the dark.

THREE WOMEN
John Currin, Stamford After-Brunch

Everyone's head's too big.
Everyone's neck's too long.
Everyone's knees are a bit too sharp.
In every way the painter's judged them wrong.

The upholstered chair crowds the upholstered couch
so the woman at right appears to have one leg
wedged between the furniture. (Ouch.)
But she grins heedlessly, a rich rag,

once a husband's shirt, knotted round her head
in a lusciously careless coiffure,
a round dome palpably echoed
by buttocks that project far past the frame to tender an insolent offer

eluding the eye, embraced by the imagination,
the dirty imagination, the jittery thrill
of this exercise in uncanny titillation.
I adore the beautiful

middle figure, blond hair pulled tight and cascading
around her stretched Bronzino throat, her smile an emblem
of occult delight. She tucks up her too-scrawny right leg
and I can discover her left leg and her right arm

nowhere. Her face betrays a gleam from nowhere,
stupidly brilliant, her serene downcast eyes
almost distracting from how, reckless of nature,
her amazing, realistic eyebrows rise

an inch too high on her forehead's cool slate.
The dark-haired woman at left laughs so hard
she squints, her hand a claw, her upper teeth
glinting in lamplight like a scalpel blade.

Clutching little cigars, martini glasses
chiming in a triad, they enjoy
a cackle at the fruits of happiness.
The room hums homey with conspiracy,

a rumbling hum shuddering safety glass,
scorching books, sparing dental evidence
from blown-up buses, holy sites, whole cities
resurrected picturesque as ruins

in coffeetable books browsed by three women
hot as fore-gossip, cool as an after-whisper,
spinning, shearing, and casting us out to moan
in an envy inevitable as winter.

THE OLD and NEW CEMETERIES
for Steve Stern

With a slow, silent clatter
like dominoes the stones
spotted with worn Hebrew
clamber over each other
as if they were prisoners
clawing up to air
over the backs of loved ones,
trampling darlings deeper
in the breathless chamber.
The stones can barely stand,
having exhausted underground
by 1792,
when Prague determined to close
this rough medieval ghetto,
the graveyard for Jews,
and dedicate a new.

A Jew goes into the ground
obeying an ancient text.
A Jew must rot in the earth
till the corpse is full perplexed
in one dusty compound.
This the bones comprehend
when newborns first gulp breath,
breath that burns like flame
or soothes the lungs like snow,
breath that begins to blow
through city and tragic wood,
whirling Eve and Adam,
each dustman and bonemaid,
back to their filthy home.
Into the ground they go.

Rabbi Löw's ancient tomb
stands a little aloof,
a crown among snaggled teeth
with a dark plot of gum around it,
a little *Totenraum*.
The rabbi composts beneath,
dutifully confounded
with other human filth.
He'd popped the letter *shin*
into the mouth of his Golem
who roared alive to avenge
Prague's docile Jewry
living among the goyim
as though behind plate glass,
a stone's throw apart,
now suddenly astounded
by their creature's gory rage—
blood for a slaughtered milk
cow or a smashed shopfront—
vicarious fury sprung
from the heart's locked attic,
now loosed from a secret page.

Ages from that neighborhood,
the new graveyard is light
and airy as a park.
Its avenues run straight,
straight stones on every block,
no crowding in shadow,
no camp or Old World ghetto.
At a much-trafficked corner
lie the bones of Kafka.

Burnt offerings, bric-a-brac,
scrawlings in demotic
American litter the grave,
each Elvis-like devotion
corrupt with naiveté
as if his corpse could hear,
as if the bones could care,
as if they held some truth
to heal the mourner's clay—
the sort of thing to drive
all Kafkas back to bed,
black covers over the head.

In the new cemetery
the empty boulevards stretch
for what seems miles, the sky
the color of sifted ash.
On the wooded alley past Kafka
the graves attain their end;
regardless of command
none comes tumbling after.
The Jews of course went away
on trains propelled by breath,
exhaust from the black earth,
an orderly transportation
no one had foreseen
and none dared prophesy,
only to return
in compounds of their own,
a gray precipitation
weightier than fog,
to other earth than Prague.

POETS' PARK, MEXICO DF

You and I risked our necks to get there, dodging
the mad cars careening around it, merging
from all angles, a condensing asteroid
swarm. Our eyes, forced open, wept in the acrid
air. Breathlessly we landed on that island
green as imagination, nearly blind
to traffic, though we heard the autos grumble.
Throughout this miniature oasis people
strolled, played with their kids, lunched. One couple necked
like no tomorrow near a less romantic
memorial to a poet I'd never heard
of. His bronze head, looking grotesquely severed,
rested on an open concrete book
as if admonishing all poets, "Look
on this life, this work, and think again:
would you choose loving under this lush green
or locking yourself up in an attic room?
The real, polluted thing? Or some daydream?"
We walked arm in arm; head after bronze head
would neither speak nor smile nor grudge a nod.
Exhilaration? Gray contentment? Anguish?
Who knew? I had no syllable of Spanish.
Emerging from the poets' sanctuary,
the car-stink stinging, our eyes again gone blurry,
we found a fountain fashioned like a pen,
its nib replenishing a pool. A fountain-
pen. I pose beside it in your photo,
writing, writing forever with clear water.

From *Enamel Eyes, A Fantasia on Paris, 1870* (2016)

Enamel Eyes is a historical fiction in the form of a multivoiced lyric sequence. It imagines the Franco-Prussian War and the siege of Paris from the perspectives of both prominent Parisians and ordinary citizens. Its large cast includes political and military figures, such as Emperor Napoleon III and Empress Eugénie; the famous artists of the period, including Degas, Manet, and others; and the real-life creators and fictional characters of the ballet *Coppélia*, which premiered May 25, 1870.

Coppélia, the great comic ballet of the nineteenth century, concerns a mad inventor who creates a female automaton. Sixteen-year-old Giuseppina Bozzacchi triumphed in the role of Swanilda, the clever village girl who discovers Coppélia's mechanical nature and wins back the love of Franz, her fiancé. She is a key character in the sequence.

Within two months, in July, France declared war on Prussia. The Second Empire collapsed when Prussian troops captured Napoleon III at Sedan on September 2, and the new government of the Third Republic determined to continue the war. As Paris fell under siege, food and medical care grew scarce. The Bois de Boulogne and Vincennes were clear-cut for heating and cooking fuel, and Parisians resorted to eating horse, household pets, and rats, while exotic animals from the zoo furnished the city's fanciest restaurants. With Paris under artillery bombardment, France capitulated in January. In March, after Prussian troops withdrew, the radical Commune took control of the city. Civil war broke out in the streets, and the increasingly conservative republican government suppressed the Communards in May 1871, finally restoring peace.

WING LIGHT

My dreams burst in flame each night till I wake
drenched in unquenching liquid. Poor Emma Livry!·
The bright dust on the butterfly's wing—ash.
Nine candles Mama'd lit upon my cake
curled up their silky wicks, crisp, black, and grisly.
With all my breath I blew them out. A flash,
Signorina Boschetti said, a wing light
caught Emma's skirt as she rehearsed the deaf
and dumb girl in some opera—not dance's
silk geometry, but ignorant mime.
Her mute screams ricocheted off paradise.

> Weeks before, she'd schooled Feydeau
> on ballet terms his novel lacked.
> He revealed his book's heroine
> dies onstage, tulle skirt having swept
>
> through the footlights, burned to ash.
> *How awful! How grim!* Emma cried.
> Then: *We dance like moths. All the same,
> fine death for any dancer.*

Panettone from La Signorina
for my birthday. Already I'm on pointe!
She's exiting Milan because La Scala
turns dancers (she says) into furniture
in tulle and greasepaint (any more panettone
and she'll be a dancing breakfront!). Join her?
Would I! And train with Madame Dominique?
A *petit rat!* The Paris Opéra!

> All onstage froze, fire and smoke
> trailed her screams, loud meteor
> till a coryphée knocked Emma down,
> beating flames out barehandedly.

Emma grabbed charred scraps of tulle
to cover up burnt nakedness.
I will come back grown up, she sighed,
not twenty-one. And France wept.

City of Flame, I'll spread my wings. They burn
to dance *Le Papillon*. I'll likewise dare
disdain the flameproofing that turns our skirts
a dingy shade of ash before the fact.
Poor Emma Livry—your death demands I dance
your apotheosis of sheer suffering
but not like I'm on fire.
                        Like fire itself.

SWANILDA WALTZES

The merest filament
links me to the firmament;
the merest nerve
renders the curve

back
of my
mirac-
ulous eye

a holy text
for the pleasures
of a wholly sexed
universe.

>   Waltzing round our village square
>   I'd love to fly off. Still she reads.
>   Such a smart girl! How can that old
>   crazy goat keep her on his string?

A rigid girl
who won't descend to waltz
revolts me, revolts
a germane world

whose seedpods
rattling in our ears
make of love no more a farce
than featherbeds.

It's Germanic! a girl who won't
come dance in the square
must have a tin ear
or a tin cunt,

such cheap metal to ignite
such chill. If she won't dance
no earthly magnet
can draw her circle far from Franz.

      Modern girls crave other girls
      to tattle truths that, locked inside,
      crack our hearts. What dark pressure cramped
      her into diamond? Fuck her.

THE EMPEROR ATTENDS *COPPÉLIA*

You must see her dance the doll,
one critic raved, *first statue-stiff,*
then a whirlwind, all grace and light.
Gautier wrote, *Her charming face*

makes us feel joy, pain, and love.
—Her thrilling hands dance full of life.
—Emma Livry reborn in spades,
simply a little marvel.

The emperor, on behalf of Terpsichore,
blessed Giuseppina's revolutionary
impersonation. Boy, could that doll dance!—
purple old guard and red republicans
all thrilled at Saint-Léon's brainy village
girl tricking the mad dollmaker; her legs
flashing, ticking like fleshy clockwork, could fool
an empire. Loud and rowdy shouts fell
from blue-collared throats, a paradisal ruckus
drowning clapping from the imperial box.

Invisibly he'd spied on her backstage
before she laid the Opéra under siege,
a new star glimmering on her audience,
forgetting the customary *révérence*
as if his box stood empty, the emperor
having vanished, which he would, come September.
Giuseppina felt like some new planet
rising in telescopes, spinning in orbit
toward the sun and reddening in rays
whose glow would last another hundred days.

THE CREATOR'S LOVE for HIS CREATION

Comedy disowns me. Embrace me, fear!
Snug in your spindle-limbs, protect me
from obstreperous romps and village fêtes,
mud-stained stockings, rain-washed hair, loud perfumes,
heaving bodices, all the operations
of arousal sanctified by superstition.

What girl would shake her wheatstalk in my ear?

Eat the fruit, and after, spread the seed.

> Spring. The girls' skirts twirl like clouds
> with dazzling sunrays underneath
> lifted hems. Brows, dark eyes, and raised
> questions I must not understand.

> Even if she doesn't scorn
> my battered top hat, cane, and limp,
> how could these gnarled, age-spotted hands
> knead young alarming white skin?

Young mountain sun and big stupid mazurkas
stir fragrances of rut, unbuttonings
in occult nooks of half-timbered rooms
on featherbeds, woolsacks, or straw,
beastly beds for scented descent.
Shadows cast under the mutable moon
catch in the casement. A few words from the mayor
and a light snack, bread and wine, say, sanctify
the scientific flow of animal spirits,
the flux of flesh under fingertips.

The village is crammed enough, I say.

> In my workshop lab I'll keep
> creating new, well-oiled machines.
> Genius takes years. I'll generate
> worlds of such fine new specimens,

dolls that dance. Now: making love.
Can cunning craft one perfect girl?
Limbs like snowdrifts, coal hair; her breast
must rise and fall like clockwork.

My lovely nerve-numbing Alps, astonish
smell and taste, freeze extremities, appall
the eyesight into crystal vision.

                Winter!

Damn the circling in the market square.
Damn small linen fluttering on the line.

One wants a girl a little cold, a girl
who loves to read, who keeps her head above
her heart. Here! consume my
                        Copernicus, darling.
One wants a girl who loves a little, daddy's
bright pupil fixing on his stare, though prone
to tearing as a cataract clouds in
to correct the light. The eye reveals God?

                Please.

I can carve her jewel-hard
and set her out where all will see
virtuous, well-read womanhood.
I don't mind she walks awkwardly.

Other girls, like animals,
want dancing. Yes, one other thing.
Read your book, brainchild, concentrate.
How far apart your legs stand!

Electric with life, exquisite moving parts
demand a delicate imagination,
fine tolerances. Lids and lashes, waltz

into her shallow eyes young fluttery men.
Let them eat grief in the keen teeth
of the machine back of her enamel eyes,
her mind calculating the measure
of raw boys drinking from them. Who
can measure up to love's Limoges?
If just one girl would stop the dance to run
her warm hand down this face, if only
the living vertex of her loving
apparatus showed not obtuseness but
an acute and open heart, if only—

Therefore here's my steel one, my Athena,
my moon, reflective darling, my Diana,
my brainchild, every goddess, my

Olympia?

Coppélia.

COPPÉLIA TELLS the FACTS of LIFE

A man peers into his brain
as into the back of
a spoon.
On reflection, they fall
in love.
And in some full
ripeness somewhat later,
after some months' sum
of labor,
I stand perfected, each limb
calibrated to inflame,
a new gadget,
I'm told, of desire: this arm,
this leg, finger, and lip,
thigh and hip, the industrial
secret of skin, a living
doll dancing
stiffly, a ratcheted
crotchet, a drizzle
of lubrication.

> Reading all day, trapped, entranced
> by books whose black marks make no sense.
> No one bids me spring up to dance;
> switch me on, that's all love demands.

> Just a touch, off fly my books
> and I will jump, jig, minuet.
> Boys who cast such long, loving looks
> can't guess the thing they might get.

I am lovely as a clock,
clean as the Arctic,
and smooth as the shock
of porcelain under the hand.
Is desire like wind in the hair?
Has it a wreath
beneath, leaves, fur?
These eyes of enamel,
though true Prussian china blue,
limit my vision. I see
feelingly. That silly boy
under the Town Hall clock,
his spoonback nose,
his mouth miming O,
a drop of liquid navigating
the down of his cheek:
he is lovely he would smile
he would caress he will dance
in time he will rise
to the necessary
miracle when I fall
from the wrought-iron rail
wreathing my balcony.

GIUSEPPINA GETS a LESSON in COURTSHIP

If Franz were not such a flirt,
if the boy were all that he promised,
my soul wouldn't wander so famished
and my heart wouldn't harbor such hurt.
But look at him, sharp in his shirt
embroidered in lovebirds, my fanciest work,
mooning, spying up under the skirt
of that bitch on the balcony, making me pissed
despite Delibes's sunny mazurka.

Can I fault him? A boy who's a girl?
The *abonnés* call La Fiocre
La belle androgyne. She's a joker
in doublet as well: she'll wheel
us about till my brain and I whirl,
then she'll kiss me *bang* on the mouth
so my breath catches and my toes curl.
And she's fiancée to a banker—
it's the wickedest city on earth!

But as Franz she's one of the boys,
the best boy, with muscular legs
and the firm rump of an Olympian page
cross-dressed in a Shakespeare disguise.
No wonder Degas loves to paint her:
she sights down that retroussé nose,
her wasp-waist demanding a dirty embrace,
her heat draws my arm hairs erect, and a faint, pure
waltz erupts in my chest. How strange.

> *Giuseppina, you're a doll;*
> *Coppélia pales. Don't worry: her*
> *steely white skin, stiff ratchets can't*
> *touch the smooth flesh North Italy*

*blessed you with. Banana nose,
black bedroom eyes: Act 3, when we
kiss on stage, my tongue takes your tongue.
Your Eugénie Fiocre.*

SWANILDA ARMS for WAR

If they dare send Franz off to war
with wide-eyed boys from wild-eyed lands,
embedding him in la belle France
like fruitless seed, I'll turn his daguerre-
otype's silver smirk and stare
to the wall. I'll turn to stone. Franz,
there's more to love than picking bones
with Prussian boys or playing with fire.

> Here's our scene: clean village square,
> an alpine land so picturesque
> war can plant no stone. Wave the flag!
> Death to Bismarck! Damn Germany!
>
> Franz, our conscript, stands for France
> (in French the names sound quite the same).
> Where'd he get that dumb German name?
> Pigheaded as the Prussians!

Ten bricks short of a load, at least,
he dreams love pricks him to the field.
The miniature that makes him shiver
like a needle north in the naked cold
marking his heart now and forever—
she or I on his bare chest?

ENDS of EMPIRE

The Empress Eugénie,
one last maid in attendance,
sloughed her finery
and dressed in a real woman's
real clothes, clandestinely
seeking passage northwest
with her American dentist.

She fled the Tuileries
in bourgeois drag. The servants
set fire to their liveries
and bagged swag. Painless Evans
was nuzzling two toothsome *filles*
when Eugénie's blushing entrance
curtailed all entertainments

of empire. In his carriage,
passing for lunatics,
they betrayed Paris to siege
and stole to the Deauville docks,
their destiny an English
asylum, their Opéra necks
redeemed by music hall tricks.

>   Only three years earlier
>   the emperor and Eugénie
>   hosted Europe's crowned heads of state:
>   France's World's Fair, proud on the Seine.

>   Glass and steel stretched all along
>   the Champ de Mars, where Prussia's gift,
>   monstrous cast-steel guns, let us see
>   war's future. *C'était trop beau.*

Louis's dainty heart would stop
too soon. The dead empire's
crown prince, pale in hope,
fell, pierced by a Zulu spear's
revolting iron tip.
Eugénie lived to ninety-four,
fifty years beyond the six-month war.

VOTIVE OFFERINGS

A blast of alpine air upon our naked
arms, nine girls tiptoed in; all of us crossed
ourselves as if invading a cathedral
and not a cranky old inventor's workshop.
Fear, like a priest, bullies us into worship.
Ranks of detached limbs hang upon the wall
like votive offerings, wood arms embraced
by nothing, wood legs dangling, knee joints crooked.

    Papa fell hard, snapped his shin.
    We bought a tin leg, which we hung
    on the church wall, prayed Mary might
    intercede. Faith paid. Papa healed.

    Silver heart next, purchased when
    my sister fell hard, broke her own;
    hard to tell just how well it's worked:
    she hasn't uttered one word.

Now, like a peacock, pampered Coppélia,
silent as a church, deep as her book,
skin sleek as steel and murderous as cannon;
in the moonlight, empty as a chalice,
eyes giving back the clarity of ice,
blood sunk under her cheek in subterranean
channels. Pinch the bitch, and—Ow! she's clockwork,
perfect in every limb, a heartless failure.

Outside our village, outside this ballet,
in the big world the war mazurkas on.
While we dance, they're dying to make us cross
ourselves. Crutches thump homeward to our gates
under shells bent on crumping us to bits.
Come, mad genius, graft limbs, make our war boys
dance. And love? If Franz falls to a machine
I pray it's my mechanical bourrée.

They've a makeshift hospital
for children who've lost limbs or worse
in the siege, gangrene, bomb debris.
Wanted: one sharp dollmaker. I

heard about one little girl
no offering can hope to save.
Prussian shell quite cut her in two
first night of the bombardment.

TRAVESTY

    Rosa Bonheur's trousers served
    her bravely: horse fairs, abbatoirs,
    tromping stench, mud, merde, blood to sketch
    horses, cows—yet no outfit called

    her to fight. Bobbed hair, Gauloises,
    she fooled the townsfolk:—*See the sweet*
    little old man? Once sang in Rome,
    St. Peter's last castrato.

Eugénie Fiocre swaggered. She'd
spent half her Opéra career in pants,
androgynous colonel thrusting with her blade,
leading her buxom squadron to romance
the shapely spouses of a backward village
whose men had run off on a drinking tour.

The hungry peasant wives, swooning onstage,
fancied Eugénie's plump posterior
a saddle fit for battle *en boudoir.*

The war made Rosa Bonheur itch to fight.
She drilled with rifles, marched with macho neighbors—
rejected! She envied Marie-Antoinette
Lix, who rose to lieutenant of sharpshooters.

As the war crossed borders into travesty,
Bonheur won her legal
battle to wear pants—not to glut her passion
for panting breasts,
not in 1870,
but to brave slaughterhouse and stableyard,
treading blood and filth as in the field:
for painting beasts.
In a single bird, *The Wounded Eagle,*
she fantasized the Prussian
army plummeting,
amazed at Rosa mailed, martyr-slender
and blazing in sun-dazzle, legendary
Joan reborn and spurring France to glory.

DAUGHTERS of INVENTION

The Prussians can't create a dancing bear
or crowing cock, no sorcerer flicking hoops
around a floozy floating in mid-air.
They can't out-engineer automatons
like ours. They settle for sending up our troops
to dance in the sky a moment before
dropping to earth, scattering in feet and hands
and scraps of uniform in scarlet rains.

Our girl has torque—the grace of a machine,
perfumed with engine oil
moistening eyes and lips, secreting a sheen
to her limbs that allow her to whirl
until she stops dead, sighting like a gun,
staring point-blank with eyes tough as enamel.
She barely stands, slouching with every step,
a demoiselle reclining standing up.

> Fear, like love, lurks deep inside
> until bombardment draws it out.
> Paris these days, turned abattoir,
> shrinks the heart, male pride curled asleep.

> Boulevard or battlefield?
> To lose your heart—how literal
> can you get? Take automatons:
> no muss—your heart remains whole.

The secret wartime government of love
quickens the improvising connoisseur
with aphrodisiac weapons that can leave
real blood on any suitor's nether hair.
The new-made whore, the borrowed bed, the grave—
the same inviting arms, the same blind stare
can lay you low as any arms of Krupp's,
this living doll, these automatic hips.

SWANILDA MEETS HER TWIN

What does it mean? What can it mean? A man
so lonely he goes mad and builds a girl
furnished with everything, and yes, I mean
everything, just look: right down to the curl
of our disputed provinces, she's my twin,
Alsace to my Lorraine, no blood but oil
for beaus who blanch, or stick at human friction.
And her eyes, miracles of darkened vision,

glow tough and glossy, unlike mine—enamel
like a tooth: I can tap them with my fingers,
click click like a machine. Mine can't dissemble
so well, though Franz ensures they're washed with tears.
He stares upon her stupid stare as simple
as a china plate, moaning and mooing. She wears
stupidity like genius: in blank reflection
her eyes shine, repulsive in attraction.

> *Even if your face gets slapped,*
> *or fingers probe you, read your book.*
> *I have made you. You can't decay.*
> *When my life work lies full revealed,*
>
> *damn the goose girls giggling round*
> *my steps through town. Come, life's delight:*
> *joy in your drop-dead china eyes,*
> *stone silence from your dead heart.*

JUST LOOKING

    Thirty-six, past army age,
    Degas enlists, right eye so bad
    target bull's-eyes flare bloodily,
    all the world sunset through his sight,

    rosy-tinged like female flesh
    when slapped, or fresh-poached from the bath,
    spied upon, some fair enemy's
    lines bright in bloody moonlight.

Morisot tattled that Manet, *mon vieux*,
said I would not know what to *do* with one.
Travesty! Slander in drag as a *bon mot*.
The clothes fly off. Before they can come on,
they're posed, flamingos in the studio.
—*Monsieur Degas's a perfect gentleman!*
Each dancer plays his goddess, not his tart.
If they dreamt how I take the beasts apart.

Commuting home from war! Near Bastion 12,
a whore came up, face dark against the sunrise,
rouged like hell. For the chump-end of a loaf
she offered nourishment to damn my eyes
but I, who won't taint looking into life,
dressed her like death and plunked her in a chaise
before the window: a portrait blood-suffused,
undone, one highlight whitening her fist.

    Working clothed, for once, inside
    his frigid, wine-dark studio,
    rigid, backlit, she looked aflame
    (fucking siege, all sight fraught with fire),

    gladly took her fee in food,
    a chunk of horse meat, quick *merci*,
    grabbed with both hands, dug in her nails,
    sank starving teeth in raw flesh.

A DEBATE about REALISM

Tissot posed British Colonel Burnaby
stretched like Olympia, under a map
of empire where the sun refused to set.
Down his long form ran an endless red stripe;
in his hand pulsed the latest cigarette.
Dazzling as a jewel, a polished breastplate
smirked at the scarlet horsehair crest atop
his regimental helmet. Its split harelip
walrus mustache lisped, *Good show! Pip-pip!*
By the fall of 1870

Tissot left drawing rooms to draw the war:
French infirmaries where comrades' wounds
puckered like kisses, and fetching portraiture
of soldier boys and canteen girls. His friends
started dying. When Cuvelier the sculptor
caught a bullet, Tissot on instinct sketched
from death—still-life as portrait. Degas raged.
—*Bringing his body back would have been better.*

    Bloody fields, now bloody town.
    The crimson paint once perfect for
    officers' red-striped trouser legs
    now becomes men shot in the street.

In Tissot's print, *The First Killed Man I Saw,*
a soldier pitches headlong down a wall
of Paris dissolving like a waterfall.
Cuvelier's unrecognizable,
a truly private man.
We don't have an opinion from Degas.
The eye that drew and fired for the Commune
forced Tissot to take off. But what would sell
in that barbaric land across the Channel?

Painting London's rich at play,
thank God for toothsome, healthy girls,
giant silk bows thrust out at you,
gift-wrapping for a round rump.

FEVER DREAM

Because I'm dancing, Paris catches fire.
A red mob threatens Notre Dame with torches—
it's like a novel by Monsieur Hugo—
but it's Our Lady they'll reduce to ashes.
My tutu twirls like sunset burning through
the rose window. Its rustle lisps like prayer.
A priest yells—no, the Communard Verlaine,
the only man without fire on the brain,

calming the crowd under Our Holy Mother
who smiles down in relief. *Sooner set
your torches to your neighbor's house,* he cries.
(*Quelle bonne idée!* they shout.) How has my mirror
sold last year's face, the scrawny *petit rat*
aged fifteen, for these stained-glass, poached-egg eyes,
this blistered cheek? I'm cratered as the moon,
toxic as coal gas swelling a balloon

rising, as I'm rising to a command
performance: Our perfect Lady—and her son.
Come dance to the bells, my bridegroom, helpless one.
Refill the shops with loaves, the Seine with fishes.
Bid the mazurkas magically ring
the populating village. Free the girl sprung
from Dr. Coppélius's clockwork madness
to heal my face with her living hand,
and darling, rise, rise with me to tread
high over Paris, soldiers, and our dead.

> *Giuseppina, keep asleep,
> enjoy your sweat-stained fever dream.
> Consciousness grants souls scant escape:
> hunger pangs, burnt flesh, children's screams.*

> *Fire will cleanse new-wakened eyes,
> combustion kidnap oxygen.
> Quick as tulle we'll all flash to smoke,
> dear, trust me. Emma Livry.*

FESTIVAL of the BELLS

    Let the town bells wag their tongues:
    to toll a tossed-out emperor.
    Knelling young men dead, Prussian guns
    ring in peace, each boy's armistice.

Clang clang, up leaps Franz!
New bells, grant loving civic
sanction; let carillons
bless Swanilda's balletic
but human swayings. Machines
shock with their lifelike
legs, but cogs and valves
can't thrill like living nerves.

    Wedding day's swift carillon
    rings hope of newborn French to help
    quicken sad steps, hands joined for our
    death-dance in grave procession.

Two bodies pledge their aging
with clear tears, not amber oil.
Neither's wired for miming—
two darlings set to fall
bedward, slant-rhyming,
pause to pay their toll,
the altar's manmade magic
drowned out by love's rough music.

Hands will chafe cold feet
and hearthfires chase all chill.
Within the snug retreat
of a cozy nuptial cell,
may ultimate defeat
tingle its lightest knell,
one alarming tongue
alarmed on mortal skin.

LE JARDIN des TUILERIES

View the ruins, barked Thomas Cook.
As English flocked, ex-Communards
wondered when they'd face firing squads.
Haute couture's Charles Worth snapped up choice

capitals, quoins, consoles from
the Tuileries for garden knick-
knacks. The town, 1883,
knocked down the stones left standing.

Evans the dentist strolled the Tuileries
communing with garden ghosts. Eugénie's
long-ago lunatic flight felt farcical
as now he watched the bird-enchanter, Pol,
delight a flock of kids. They'd not been born, they
never had brawled for the rights to a scrawny
pigeon to feed their family for a week.
These children laughed, watching the fat birds peck
and bobble up and back, mechanical
as dolls. Evans recalled a summons to pull
a festering bicuspid from the empress's
dainty mouth. Le Palais des Tuileries
brooked no decay—perfume embalmed her pain;
his roused nostrils jolted his American
uprightness. Who'd imagined he'd uproot
the empress, waltzing her to a little boat?
He could sail home—and waste his artistry
on yahoos? Long live aristocracy!
The pigeons danced a czardas around the palace
Paris had torched for democracy—no trace
of strutting kings (or emperors) of France,
but flowers, ash paths, no trace even of ruins.

SEVENTEEN at LAST

Epidemics prowled the town
to prey on old, poor, crippled, sick
citizens. Most trained doctors stitched
at the front. Young things coughed up blood,

ballet girls thrown out of work,
no francs for food. Stars waltzed away
from the sky, last dance partnered by
diphtheria or smallpox.

Now étoile of the Opéra Ballet,
Giuseppina asked, "Am I young or old?"
the morning of her seventeenth birthday.

Her pointes had stabbed the lewdest *abonné*
out of his dreams such lightness could be sold.
Once étoile of the Opéra Ballet

blazing through Paris, now she knelt to pray:
Will no one love me till my bones grow cold?
This morning, on her seventeenth birthday,

something squeezed her extraordinary clay,
seizing in a burning stranglehold
this étoile of the Opéra Ballet.

Degas, immortalizing her bourrée,
cast her in wax. As brazen cannon rolled
the morning of her seventeenth birthday,

she heard a mazurka beginning to bray,
a star falling out of fever. Bells tolled
this étoile of the Opéra Ballet
the morning of her seventeenth birthday.

Loving in Truth: *New Poems*

> But wherefore says she not she is unjust?
> And wherefore say not I that I am old?
> O, love's best habit is in seeming trust,
> And age in love loves not to have years told.
> > Therefore I lie with her, and she with me,
> > And in our faults by lies we flattered be.
>
> —SONNET 138

1. The Penny Poems

ALL the SAME

Spinning *Cosi,* Penny ponders. "Mozart
slays me. I'd fall for a guy aged 250
who understood a girl like Fiordiligi.
What the heart hurts to learn! If I lose heart
God let me lose it to a man whose art
seduces me with such sincerity
that even when it lies—say, poetry
concocted by some Don Giovanni upstart—
I might pretend his groaning sonnet's genuine,
scrawled straight from a vein. Such artful designs
can make me lie, my feelings (or myself) full peeled.
Such joy, conceiving plots to bare our ends.
All the same, meeting you on that softball field,
boy, I could swear that you were born Albanian."

MUSING

How many poets have sung this photograph!
Serious Penny, musing at fifteen,
Keats labeled an unravished bride, and Donne
conceived with cardigan and blouse tossed off.
Arnold knelt on naked Dover Beach
where pruny Eliot offered her a peach.
Pricked on by his general of hot love
Shakespeare lurched into the breach. Tennyson
made her his Maud, Chaucer his Alisoun.
I've scribbled her a poem or two myself,
fool's gold plating the tribute of the ages:
a six-foot shelf of sixty thousand pages
singing how this snapshot of my inchoate
darling has launched a thousand odes, a poem
from every bard except the *Beowulf* poet,
who never sang a girl but Grendel's mom.

THE GARDEN

"God," says Penny, "it's so much work,
dividing iris, staking columbine,
I'll never get it done in time."
In time for what? "Before it's dark.
Look: already 6 PM
and all these weeds—if I don't pluck
them now, they'll overrun
the flowers and tomatoes. Come
help me spread grass clippings round
the stems." Stumbling towards fall,
the lettuce long bolted, tiger lilies toil
for us, tantalizing the blurred
buzz-beat of the hummingbird.
Green goes red as tomatoes haul
their branches down to earth.
Plucking their leathery warmth
to slice and sprinkle with good oil
and a sharp splash of vinegar,
she says, "I haven't done enough.
God, these taste so wonderful.
I've really got to work next year."

HOLES in the PICTURE

Let's look for reality naked
eyes can't see, say, through the hole
where a ruby or darkling pearl
should hang, or in the loose-laced placket
gaping to mark a happily pregnant
prophet, convert, saint or sibyl.
Holes in the fabric rapture a girl
out of her clear skin, beauty painted
as if the veil of things has torn
under the knifepoint of our nervous
stalking. As a Flemish Magdalen
prays, a penetrating flash:
any world beyond flesh
still must cleave to nakedness.

DYEING

Color your hair, darling, if you must.
Dye it the red of cabernet or blood
and hide the gray lights glowing in your head
like emanations from a future ghost,
neural mandates from the skull embossed
upon your darker curls. I will abide
your dyeing as long as it cheats the dead,
and love you nonetheless. Yet having kissed
your graying part, and studied open-eyed
and, at midnight, by lovers' braille, I'll stand
forth ready to recite your body blind.
When our curves falter, flagging with gravity,
we'll pass with flying colors, grayed or dyed,
advanced love granting its advanced degree.

THE GOOD DEATH

"When do those someday-blessed in Purgatory
get to see God face-to-face?" asks Penny.
Her q's not personal, but academic,
not quite angels flirting with Terpsichore
on pins, but Rogier van der Weyden's triptych—
"Those rays shooting from Christ's head? No holy gimmick,
but radar to the widow of Jean Braque
her masses and indulgences would work."

Prayers are bribes, decreed the Council of Florence,
promoting the dead, like grade school. If you haggled,
your ducats could chop centuries from the sentence,
speeding husbands to beatific visions
like Rogier's electric Christ. Or in Baghdad
a split-second before the blast, the virgins
dancing in the head of a fanatical man
who dreams, like us, the best death is the small one.

JANUARY

At last the living room rolls back
from holy night to starless day, your
Christmas crèches packed away for
the lengthening months. Adios, tin cac-
tus, flip-up backdrop for our bladelike
sheet-tin *Jesús,* God's little razor.
Au revoir, madame outside the manger
with two cats to bless *bébé,* one black,
one white. Arrivederci, paisan',
dancing reverently with your bear.
Magi, Mary, Ox and Ass, go
up to the attic for hibernation,
when dreams shall prophesy your rescue,
a newborn life next shrunken year.

CORPUS CHRISTI

The Blessed Virgin floated through the streets
despite her heavy hair and silver crown,
despite the punishing Sevilla heat's
hellfire highs, breaking all laws for late June.
An embroidered velvet cloak weighing her down
sweltered three boys under its humid skirts
who, charged with sailing her erect through town,
learned how passion, divine or human, hurts.
Two elegant *señoras* served us scraps
we barely could digest, of local lore,
how soldiers once rode horses up the ramps
of the cathedral tower in ranks of four,
which left us wondering how we might discourse
on why you'd climb a tower on a horse.

A NEW LOVER

"You won't be*lieve* what Rogier did last night,"
sighed Penny, stretching like an odalisque.
Where was I? Rogier, clever as any cat,
is batting the dangling shade-pulls. "He circles
me, with his nose never leaving my body.
It was so delicate, so . . . so erotic."

I'd slept through this romance of 5 AM.
"And he kept licking constantly, but lightly,
with his raspy tongue." Off in some other dream,
I've missed my life, again. "And he never bit me"—
as she curved me a glance that slid from Titian's
Venus to Manet's Olympia—"not once."

PENNY AND THE BEAR

When Penny met the bear along the path,
the interview left little chance for banter.
Fifteen green feet off, she watched it rear
on thick hind legs, a full six feet, its teeth
bared, snout periscoping around to sniff
the strange, suddenly populated air.
Her brain madly rummaged through TV nature
programs: should she drop flat, rehearsing death?
For that she felt unready. Should she scream?
Her voice had fled: the merest human racket
lay beyond her. Should she loom gigantic,
hoisting high overhead her hooded jacket?
She couldn't move a muscle, a stratagem
that signaled it to mosey off, this time.

TORTUGAS

The body of Christ, oiled and dressed
in luscious robes for the feast-
day and paraded through the street,
left all the hungry host knocked out
save the toddler wriggling in her papa's
arms, reaching hands out for your breast.
Her father blushed and laughed. "Tortugas!"
he said into his girl's wide eyes—
the turtles printed on your dress
or hiding under its silk disguise?
Christ hurried past us to get nailed,
a blue note in this comedy
whose other players, safely shelled
like turtles, stare in sympathy.
When Mary nurses Christ her eyes
look down, disguising all she knows,
comic relief cross-dressed as death.
Lie down, darling, while I praise
tortugas with my shorter breath
as long grass spins our last disguise,
before we're clocked like Aeschylus
by turtles hurtling from the blue.

THE PROTESTANT CEMETERY

We couldn't blame the cemetery, though
the stones of Brits and Yankees far from home
made Penny philosophical in Rome.
We'd come of course to visit Keats. Here no
tone sounded sweet as his "no tone," till—*meow*—
in floated a black cat who looked the same
as ours, who'd died just weeks before. So tame
he rubbed against her leg. "I miss him so."
Arriving in Freiburg we bought a
crouching cat in terra cotta
to plant in our yard, a stone
among creeping myrtle, guarding Otto,
who made my darling's bright eyes shine
far more than one whose name was writ in water.

PUNTA MARINA

The Jersey shore of Italy,
no women topless by the water,
its air of humid modesty
hung heavily on Penny's daughter

and heavier on her son. That night
in the square's al fresco ring
the local pride, a bantamweight,
thrilled the mob by pummeling

a young Slovakian. At three
we woke to flashing lights and screams.
A Fiat parked two cars away
from ours sat swimming in flames.

Her son slept on. He wouldn't believe
our news next morning: the scrubbed street shone.
Penny kissed me. "Go down, love,
you start the car. Then we'll get in."

RESEARCH ASSISTANT

> He gazed and gazed and gazed and gazed,
> Amazed, amazed, amazed, amazed.
> —ROBERT BROWNING

A serious iconographic purpose
underlying twin exposés, of power
women have wielded through their nether hair,
and of Christ's human nature—he's one of us
because that thicket marks his mortal focus—
prompts Penny to enlist her son, at thir-
teen half-kid, half-satyr, to prowl each floor
of the museum for signs of sprouting pubis.
It's an ingenious scheme: at once unbored,
he eyeballs every painting. Her research
advances crux by hairy crux, his reward
the tingling oils that make him buzz, "P. H.
in the 9th, 12th, 13th, and 23rd
galleries"—his Sunday school, her church.

PENNY MOURNS the RASPBERRIES

Hiking up on the north side of our road
we found the guy we'd hired to thin the woodlot
had skidded through our raspberries and plowed
the bushes under. "I guess I forgot,"
he said. "Don't worry. That's what I once did
to my wife's raspberries. Boy, was she mad!
But they'll grow back again before you know it."
Watching the sun descend in Penny's eyes,
I tasted elegies: *They won't grow back,
nothing will ever come back as it was
or ever taste so sweet.* I'd watched her dad,
trussed up in tubes, smile through his final week,
her mom, in bed, project a gray Alzheimer
vacancy, years back. Nothing ever after.
"It's all about the raspberries," she said.

STRAGGLERS

We've passed into the hell of the second rate:
Follower of Bosch, the label hopes.
"Distant follower," Penny says. "A straggler!"
and a new term for our glossary, the Secret
History of Western Art, pops
into being, joining, say, the Boobooists,
the school that paints such cutesy little Christs
with such blond, curly hair, you have to gag or
give in. We're members! Our granddaughter Ellie's
curls consecrate our every room like icons,
in snapshots primed to plunk us on our knees.
She harries the cats; we follow with our Nikons,
Ellie leading the chase, Penny the straggler
toddling behind her animated pace.

LEGACY

Benjamin, eighteen months,
fussed at Beech-Nut squash and peas,
squirmed and ducked strained legumes.
Bass and synth, *Billie Jean*'s
purring panther dance strains
sprang from FM eulogies.
Sidelong grin, dance-floor moves,
nailing smooth his high-chair bounce
left twice, twice right,
eyes shifting, each shoulder
leading, subtle *épaulement*,
slurping spoons of lentils, corn,
Billie Jean's not my lover,
Michael breathless, fading out.

DOUBLE WAKING

So anxious to get born, one broke his water
while the other somersaulted further
adrift, absconding with his private ocean.
Tiny, yes, but both elementally human,
Joseph yanked into our world a bare minute
after Mateo, his bare brother, both in it
for life now. Penny's daughter, in her bed
next door to the ward nursery, woke and heard
Mateo yowl. "Oh, my little sweetheart,"
she moaned, in tones that rolled my own grown heart
till *crack*. That night I woke to find Mateo
asleep beside me, his head on my pillow,
his lips pressed in an improbable smile,
his gnomic face scrunched up, a furling sail;
then, in an impossible clambering over
Penny to bunk between us came Joseph.
We watched them breathe the strange thin atmosphere
till I woke again, the breaking of our
liquid lives on a sharp edge out there waiting,
a waking from our dream of our awaking.

AT the WAR MUSEUM

Even with hers grown up, she's never not
a mother, viewing *Children of the Blitz,*
words written by evacuated kids:
"Today I gathered eggs warm from the nest
and didn't break one." Her eyes magnify, moist
with the elixir that can't save the world.
A card scribbled en route to Canada—
"The captain is so nice. Tonight we ate
at his table, and for our sweet had custard!"—
found waterlogged, weeks after the torpedo—
"and Mummy, I haven't once got seasick yet!"

BIRTHDAY in MIDDLE AGE

Pricing grave plots taught us the health codes, fixed as
laws of elementary physics: no two
bodies occupying a single space, so
      everywhere's nowhere;

nowhere grants Donne's private eternal jointure:
death does part, one customer to a bed, no
contract worth the flesh it's imprinted on. Well,
      so much for marriage.

Once I called deciduous autumn's trash a
blazing carpet damping our steps. Dear children,
years apart, or after a plane crash, toss us
      both in a furnace,

render us to ashes to make us clean fill,
bonedust, indistinguishable. My darlings,
don't dare stow us under a tablet carved with
      relevant data;

take our baggie into the Adirondacks;
scatter our detritus around the cabin
we constructed over the grave of one that
      tumbled beneath that

record snowfall, tamp us below your footsteps,
figure us invisibly in the carpet,
urging grass to cushion the bobcat's walk, the
      grandchildren's prowling.

OLD SNAPSHOTS

They're mail from the past
sorted in dark albums,
confined by ancient paste
and scalloped white frames

dog-eared and perforated
like monstrous postage stamps
that once commemorated
family triumphs—

a gray anniversary,
the new gray Pontiac,
the fifth birthday party
and its asthma attack.

Without denomination,
they're curious currency,
not tender except in
their mark on memory,

with no cancellation
from the past. Here, a tissue:
the eyes can still burn
as on first day of issue.

And so I peer through
a magnifying glass
at this snapshot of you.
No watermark or crease

foxes your smooth skin.
We've come face to face.
Your cardigan,
your starched blouse

with its Peter Pan collar,
and the captive light
in your schoolgirl stare
all commemorate

your polychrome simmer:
under gray adolescence,
your dormant era
whose foreign correspondence

of a life just begun
posts the mystery
of the past, in your skin
abiding beside me

at this forwarding address
where all you are
delivers late news
of all you were.

2. Side Issue

> Eve is no side issue when it comes to explanations for the Fall....
> —PENNY HOWELL JOLLY, *Made in God's Image?*

BEGINNING

A week in Italy
makes one free to
adore divinity
in Orvieto

where the tang of astringent
bianco at a caffe
cuts sharp as legend
in Maitani's relief

on the Duomo façade.
His sixteen-pointed sun
eclipsed by God
bears down

on his little clay planet.
Stars on his shoulder
show day chased by night.
Spirit over water

beats wings, a dove
with a streamlined heart,
carved marble to give
us a fitting stone start.

Gazing at the moon
the sun falls in love

as if with its own bone,
a reflection of

flame, God's delight,
his delicious earth
a blue-ribbon dessert
set to go off.

CHAOS THEORY

Create form, create division.
First light split a universe
perplexed by orientation.
The formerly formless chaos

cradled everything,
darkly pregnant with a world
entropic as a late de Kooning.
The haughty firmament pulled

out and lorded it over the seas;
sun, moon, and stars dawdled
above the docile beasts.
Hierarchic spheres and ordered

days made us despair: so beautiful,
so much like art.
Form wrestled energy, its angel.
Eve decided she needed fruit.

The world, thank God, runs down:
each melting glacier, cooling star
signals our return
to randomness, room temperature,

evening: a steady state
relieved of form, a Big Un-bang.
Goodnight, discord who made us light.
Dear darkness, make one everything.

DAY FIVE

The river ripples like marble
breaking in draperies.
The fish model the water
diaphanously in waves.

Cod and dolphin dance
through the sculpted stream.
The lobster snaps its pincers
in geologic time,

and great whales vocalize,
trembling the fishes' blood,
but the song warms their scales
and leaves them comforted.

Barracuda and shark
gorge on algaes and kelps;
the eagle and the hawk
sink talons into grapes.

Songbirds trill in stone,
each perched in a little tree
carved for it alone,
like a stalk of broccoli

above the serpentine waters
where the hand of God conducts
his universe of creatures
conceiving their good eggs.

One tree like a woman,
slinky under its bark,
dangles its nutrition
all day, and after dark,

suspending fruit so peaceful
no predator comes near;
seas full of fish, trees full
of birds in their fruitful hair.

FORESIGHT

Curious how God does
things out of curiosity,
like bringing Adam animals
to see how he'll identify

them, the crazy names
he'll dream up. God should know
he'll call these marmosets, those camels,
before Adam even o-

pens his mouth. Pleasure
grows from foreknowledge.
Anticipating closure—
this aria, that kiss—

with no distraction of surprise
makes us feel fulfilled.
It pleases
God no end to see the world

elect what he knows it will enact—
naming, snake charming,
eating plucked
fruit, hiding, lying. Never squirming,

he keeps a jealous watch over
each mite on each eyelash, each flower
knocking with pollen, each lover
mortally sick, each cure-

less virus, each war,
each geological disaster,
each and every creature
dying for another.

OPEN HEART

Eden, we have a problem.
They paraded snuffling and snarling
and so the man named them;
not one did he call *Darling*.

Lion, horse, camel, goat
tickled but pricked no purring
under his ribs, so his throat
still stuck at *Darling*,

a name God could never invent,
liquid on his heart,
good as *Firmament;*
and blinding as *Light*.

A sleep came over him.
Are you my Darling?
He fell in a dream.
Are you my Darling?

Fingertips cleft flesh.
Left hand teased out a rib
lunar and bare, without a stitch
he healed with nary a scab.

We dream of a bright bone
stepping from our chest
to worship as our own,
arm circling our waist.

We dream a primal tree
dangling the heart like fruit,
of plucking a bloody bough,
of someplace to start.

Nothing says desire
like thoracic surgery:
a scalpel for the sculptor
who cuts us. We're history.

SIDE ISSUE

At Orvieto adolescent
Eve emerges, born fifteen
and set to blossom. God omniscient
sees men fall for younger women

with breasts like figure skater's buds
that have no nurslings to distend them;
the no-man's-road that no hand hides
maps her shameless bare pudendum.

God's left hand perfects her shoulder.
Adam sleeps, his arms crossed,
hiding his physique. He's older,
possessed of a more manly chest.

Eve's magnetized by God's stark stare
drawing her body and making her cock
her head his way. She puts on power,
a splash of aphrodisiac.

There they parley eye to eye;
her right hand worries the humble ground
while her left hand strums her thigh.
Like God's, her cunning hair is curled.

She notices how God's divine
manlike thigh distends his robe.
She falls for him. She will for man
as well, in microcosmic love.

Stare gone blank, adoring God
who beams upon her sunning face,
she dabbles her toes in Adam's side.
She'll dapple blood through Paradise!

Two angels troll across the blue;
one asks if it's a good idea,
this bone-girl hot for deity.
The other's face is hacked away.

TEMPTATION

Eve stands in contrapposto,
paganly heroic.
Adam lounges, legs crossed.
His left hand fondles the bark.

She stares stark as an angel,
her face ignorant with love.
He studies the tree in profile.
His right arm's broken off.

The tree of changeless fruit
is grateful for the massage.
Ragged at the root,
ripe for sabotage,

it lifts its leaves to God,
knowing the awful burden
of data overspread
with greenness, overladen

with fruit longing to drop.
It yearns for us to taste.
Even trees live in hope.
Eve's hand offers her breast.

God points with his righteous hand
as if they can be stopped.
Doesn't he see the end?
His left hand wrote the script.

Temptation. It's a puzzle.
The thing you least want taken
you leave upon a table
in the middle of your garden.

One angel in a gauzy gown
clasps hands in prayer;
the other, speaking from the stone,
considers trial and error.

Sterile lab assistants
with a mission to spy on us,
they conduct one-way experiments
for the sake of pure science.

They're babies, say the heavenly ones,
weighed down with a human heart,
an extenuating circumstance
they'll note in their report.

IN HIDING

They've ferreted out an angle
in the great green garden,
assuming its geometry
to hide from the angel
or minister calling
in that black bullhorn basso.
The stern hand of heaven
is loving as a tree
whose blushing has begun,
its shameful leaves falling.

He once stood guard personally,
kapo of the compound,
waggling a father's finger.
Cruel trials of surgery;
nightmares for anesthetic.
Experiments no longer.
He's withdrawn. Clouds abound,
through which his fluids water
a thirsty firmament.
Eden has shrunk.

Adam and Eve crouch
cold as amphibians,
though Adam's thickened thigh
and the fulcrum of his crotch
attest he's no frog
with a jewel behind his brow:
the trembling of his leg's veins,
the twitching of his eye.
Eve lays her arm on Adam's
like fuel, log on log.

What price for knowledge
cruel as the grave
and cunning as ripe fruit?
Harvest is luscious carnage,
cloying but spurring our wants,
a dull thud at the heart
stupid as a knife
sawing a tree at the root.
We kill ourselves for love
and eat the evidence.

Eve shields her virginal face
from the gnostic radiance.
Her palms are scored with lines
like a chimpanzee's;
her twisted mouth cries *Stop*.
In the passionate embrace
of the fatherland they squeeze
into their coffin space
behind some barbarous trees.
In time they will burn up.

FALL

Eve and Adam go
to a dance,
a courtly fandango,
no chaperones,

hand to hand, hot glances,
cool steps; the muscle
in Adam's calf tenses;
Eve throws back a shoulder

while one supple leg coyly
coils around the other.
Carlo Blasis,
Italian dancing master

and author of sober books
on the subject, would mention
that exchange of amorous looks,
the certain immodest motion

in the hips while dancing,
the way their breasts press
together, as if commencing
"the final embrace."

The angels have gone where?
Changing their gowns?
Shedding coats of gossamer
for flames?

This is just the start
of the end. The tree
has shed its part-
ridges and lovebirds, who spy

from every prurient bush
on this Valentine's dance,
this coarse subterfuge
for the intercourse of hands

passing subtle fruit:
peach, pear, or tangelo,
fig or pomegranate,
clementine or mineola

(scholars disagree);
maybe a cantaloupe or a
cherry tragedy;
an apple opera.

A hissing vine coils
around the tree trunk,
grinning through its scales
with its scissory tongue,

casting a marble eye
on the First Lady
(it glows like the cherry
on a hot fudge sundae).

Stamp! Stamp on the ground!
Where is God,
who's generally around?
He's letting things slide:

the rivers escape
to the earth's four corners.
The tree will dry up
and love will abandon us

to harvest our thorns
and thistles. And fruit
shall render our bones
compliant and mute.

END of the AFFAIR

Eden's on fire! A ring of flame
shimmies like a conga line
drunk at a bar mitzvah. Shame.
Looks like hell. The tree stands alone

(heigh-ho), no birds build in its boughs.
The fruit it brings forth rots untasted.
A second tree, mysterious,
clings to life. Leaves hang blasted.

On two hawk wings the angel flies;
two more wings flutter like bridal lace.
A third pair clings to stocky thighs
like Aunt Rose in her mermaid dress.

The samurai-angel whirls a sword,
his wrist a universal joint,
his chest a rebus of the world,
his hair steel, his eyes flint.

A second angel serves as usher
bouncing the falling, gluttonous guests.
One guy screams and grips his crotch;
his wife clasps hands upon her breasts.

She can't recall how she came bare.
She stares straight forward, stunned by sin,
appalled by the delicious air
naked on her humid skin.

DEATH'S SYMPATHY

He felt bad for them—not guilty, just bad
enough to offer them some stately twangling
on his ukulele as they left, straggling
as in a funeral dance. He'd play their guide,
helping them choose their rest stops while they cried
tears, naturally; he'd boost their pride, rankling
with rejection; he'd help the poor guy drudging—
he'd shovel, jawboning side by side, same side
his wife sprang from, supermodel-gaunt, bone-
thin then, now *zaftig*, apple-cheeked, windfall-
fed. But their endless busywork! Toil, spin,
each day wasted in digging a deeper hole—
for what? Let her keep cooing at their son
nursing, the one he'd heard them call, yes, Cain.

CAIN'S GIFT

The blood cried up from the ground
and the air held its breath,
the earth's sunset-stained
face now an epitaph
for Abel's head and hands
thrust up from the grave,
that childish face profiled,
those hands clasped, a child

imagined by the sculptor
petitioning the God
who'd let the model murder
play out unimpeded.
From brother to his keeper
the singing from the sod
rose, a sunset lark
whose quavers left their mark

on Cain's consciousness,
setting him aquiver
at walking the cooling face
of earth, banished forever
from Salisbury's Chapter House,
a period put to his chapter,
and from the good book hurled
out to beget the world.

3. Loving in Truth

IN the KING'S ARMS

The most beautiful barmaid in London
    pulls my delectable nectar.
    I sip from her hand best bitter.
I drink her thrilling low rustle, *Two pound and
forty;* black satin sighs on
        her forearm's
tendon.
    I gulp my Pride; she breaks my fiver.
    Her scarlet-nailed finger
        makes me change. City suits
            swill with the Animals, drink with the Kinks.
Their poison
        cloud condenses from a gross
        of cigarettes into a nimbus
round her head. I'm undone
        by her spark
upon my palm, undone
            by her black hair's current, her dark
        eye alight in the King's
    Arms.

Boucher painted Mademoiselle O'Murphy
    tirelessly
    sprawled on her belly,
a yummy trophy
    Marshmallow Peep-
    pink, a bunny blinking up
        to Louis offstage, teenybopper thighs
            inching apart
    upon the satin sheet to dramatize
    her reverend rump.
        Now (as I like to tell my wife in galleries)
            that's what I call art.

On break she drags one deep. Down along
her long
back her underthong
    tattles earthward
        into her jeans, all
           heaven perched on a barstool,
              eternity clothed in an afternoon,
            her mouth contracting round
                her cigarette and a stunningly
    mundane smoky torrent
                  of gossip. Aroma
                  bathes me like dark over
                    the earth. *What's yours?* she insinuates nightly
laboring
        in the King's Arms, not mine.

THE LITTLE BLACK BOY

His name was Jerry Joseph. He was the first
black boy I knew. Those days we called them Negroes.
We both were four at Lake Playskool, immersed,
but not in roughhouse like the other boys.

He frightened all the little girls away
from the girl department of the big playroom.
He sat me down at their little vanity
and dabbed my cheeks from a jar of cold cream,

crowing, "We must make you bee-you-tee-full,"
working the cream in with sandpaper fingers.
Upon my face it felt thick, white, and cool.
It tingled beneath, strangely dangerous.

Then came his turn to sit upon the stool,
and though I rubbed and rubbed the white cream in
and labored to render him bee-you-tee-full,
I saw no paling of his chocolate skin,
                                          no paling of his skin.

FIRST NEGATIVE

You can't see anything beyond the window
whose opaque panes, black as volcanic glass,
have faded like memory to sepia.
The window, not the vista, is the news,

a quantum of the world made negative
and fixed on paper soused with chemicals
at Lacock, August 1835.
Bituminous diamonds lined up on diagonals

like a night-vision through an insect eye
or cottages in a utopian
village, the obsidian lights defy
the light, while day streams through the brilliant mullions

to coruscate around the velvety panes—
200 in number, Fox Talbot wrote,
could be counted with help of a lens:
a window to be looked not through but at.

But here's the actual transparent window
distracting you with eulogies to sight
and color. Facing panes no longer blind, no
longer blank, you watch yourself look not at

but *out:* the oak, the vast lawn's sudden green,
light lighting leaves, a broom, an iron gate,
your love posed in a shock of sky and stone,
a sweep not of wall but of the infinite.

TIME OUT
for Mary Jablonski

The End, concludes the photograph.
Ever after happy. But who lives?
We pretend it's a well-made narrative
some fairy godmother knocks into shape,
the photo just another halfway house,
one more lucky sublimated climax
in our recovery from growing up,
our journey to the ultimate coldframe.
We're walled out, redeemed from all that flux,
the flux that lets us solder day to day,
and we throb like a lone panel plucked out
of its comical context, Clark Kent caught
with supertrousers down, or Archie's eyes
dilating as he palms Jughead a joint.
Moments distilled from life never make sense,
neither come-hither smiles nor go-to-hell eyes.
Without the timely sinews of Meanwhiles,
breadcrumbs trailing behind us in the woods
provide no more than lunch for a speechless crow.
We wouldn't know our house if we tasted it.
Over and over we stand in isolation,
frostbitten hands frozen on our watches,
fall fashion colors charmed to shades of gray,
monochrome maple leaves hung up in mid-fall,
hovering weakly like bleak hummingbirds.
Sleep strikes the ear a far way off, a chime,
a proposition heard once in a dream
to link days fluid with desire, a stream
we dreamt once once upon a time.

THE BURIED FUTURE

Just when I seek my future it becomes
the past. It cons me everywhere I go:
it hovers an inch before my eyes, socks
me in the nose—*bang*—then it vanishes
into the swamp, my hall of records, next
to P, which brings back Q as from the dead,
and here you are, I'm hunting you, old friend,
or stalking you, ancient love, while off you go,
raising the dust on zombie highways, catching
the special out of a torndown terminal.
Elusive future, unexhumable,
I'm rummaging through my dark box of photos:
why is Daddy smiling? The marble clicks,
it strikes a claque of marbles, a chain of pictures
unprintable and unforgettable,
a wallet burning in a secret pocket:
the Buick charging off, my mother flicking
a knife through a new tan Brooks Brothers suit,
a prospect of endless sky in monochrome.
The future turns up any second. One dawn
staring hungover into eyes I saw
blackness at the sparkling irises' core,
like gazing into a camera, a dark
stupid chamber with nothing on its mind
but bearing negatives into the future—
farewell, wife; cancel those enlargements, please—
a stupid future I've kept staring into,
this rotting box of memory, my life,
taking the future as it comes and goes.

ONE-LINER

One solitary line to Ginevra de'Benci
survives from all those poems guys would write her,
for a girl who sat for Leonardo da Vinci

a legacy dishearteningly stingy:
I beg forgiveness. Love your mountain tiger.
What kind of stupid line, Ginevra de'Benci

wondered, is that? Betrothed, not yet sixteen, she
narrowed her eyes and set her wide lips tighter
than the curls lionized by Leonardo da Vinci

in her gold mane, hairs fetishized by men she
suffered to croon to her that stiff one-liner.
What *was* the line on this Ginevra de'Benci?

mused Leonardo. Who was this moon-faced wench he
had to immortalize? Merely a minor
masterpiece for Leonardo da Vinci.

Her insolent pubescence made him cringe: she
lurks in his dark juniper like a spider
conceiving gossamer—Ginevra de'Benci
endlessly sitting for Leonardo da Vinci.

HIGHER CRITICISM

The P-text and the J-text,
the J-text and the P-text;
the P-text is the post-text
while the J-text is the pre-text.

The P-text makes us two-sexed
while submission is the subtext
for the woman in the J-text,
so the J-text is the sir-text.

The female in the P-text
goes bony in the J-text;
the J-text is the ur-text,
but neither's much a her-text.

Then Eve gets quite perplexed
by the serpent in the J-text,
so the J-text's a dismay-text
while the P-text's an okay text.

The Creator grows full vexed
in the J-text, not the P-text,
so historical context
makes the J-text the key text.

The P-text is the new text
while the J-text is the first text.
The P-text is the bless-text
but the J-text is the curse-text.

The J-text is the blame-text
and the day text is the P-text;
the P-text is the post-text
but the J-text is the pretext.

WAKING to the *ENIGMA VARIATIONS*

Stumble from sleep, search for certainties:
may the left leg's new numbness disappear,
may the feet descending encounter floor,
may the gray fog encrypting morning rise

from the shock-blue clarity. Not yet. Dawdle
under the comforter, disoriented
by the stung world outside the Victorian bed,
unsnug, intolerant of this lush fiddle

section rising, plunging, a bobbing up
and back of mind on music. Mother's here;
no, shadow. When a suddenly swung door
invites you out upon the air, don't step

in momentary rapture: this is Elgar,
not Tschaikovsky: scattered singed papers, scrawled
sell orders and love notes strew the ash field,
and melancholy, towering in a major

key, Tennysonian in its belief,
our resolution stirred to daily war
like coffee. Prick on, protein, caffeine, empire!
Come, martial music: let's shave. Let us brush our teeth.

MY COMPUTER READS ME a POEM

>...poems written by a typewriter on a typewriter.
>—RANDALL JARRELL

No, I wasn't nuts or hallucinating.
In a nasal masculine voice my laptop
read my words mechanically, spilling out its
    digital guts, like

waking up and hearing my cat speak Shakespeare.
Once-embodied words in a disembodied
cancer-of-the-larynx prosthetic tone zoned
    in from the ether,

chug-a-chugging, pausing for punctuation
like a blind man balking at curbstones. Question
marks made final syllables rise, like students
    reading aloud on

autopilot: "classi*cal?*"—droning on, no
poet needed, no expressiveness wanted,
hellbent for the finish line. Page proof read, it
    chanted the time and

spelled my name, deleting all sound of "Rogoff,"
zapped from verbal memory, lost at *12 hours
57 minutes and zero seconds.*
    Hush. And then: *PM.*

WITNESS

While waiting for you to take a leak
I turned from John the Baptist's bust
and saw a tear run down his cheek

in one of Florence's less chic
museums, sculptures downed with dust.
While waiting for you to take a leak

I saw it, a descending streak—
a miracle. How could I trust
that tear down John the Baptist's cheek?

Well, neither he nor I could speak.
I might have seen a mite—I must!—
while waiting for you to take a leak,

or spider, with a silent shriek;
for exiting, when I discussed
the tear on St. John's rundown cheek,

you looked as if I gushed in Greek,
hairshirted, munching locusts, just
because you chose to take a leak
while tears ran down the statue's cheek.

THE WILTON DIPTYCH

Angels are impossible. Just take
this one, my wife's darling. Also mine,
arms crossed, a smart smirk skeptical for heaven.
A colleague's arm massaging that slender back
can't mollify this beauty. One wants a lack
(the breastless chest) of any gendered pronoun.
This set of angels, decked in dainty fingers,
soft curls, moist mouths, and supermodel figures,
includes no members. Null. Our pornographic
imagination, even the dusty take
of antiquated doctors of the church,
transplants the heart from its sequestered nook:
bursting in flame where anyone can look—
on your sleeve! White harts loll like odalisques
on blue, ambiguous but flatly committed
angel breasts, to welcome England's Richard.
He kneels to Mary, each human and gendered,
begotten into generation and wedded
beyond all biblical performance, one
knowing nothing touching his queen,
one nothing known on earth could help conceive.
Our darker knowledge doesn't make us better
than those death's chastity has thrown together
in an ultimate painting, a final take,
both quaintly pricked by fate, picked out to burn
among wings rising like blue flames, like love.

CONSUMPTION
after Schiele

Under the reign of elbow and teeth, knee
and knuckle, sapped of strength to pray,
of strength to prey, we've started to consume
ourselves: farewell, soft loving flesh, farewell,
rank and spongy organs. We're streamlining
for final nakedness, this pubic hair
one last extravagance of spiky fashion.
The Clothed One alone affords a cape, a hood,
a grin, and though we're scanty pickings, he
wraps himself around our family
gone shimmery with swirling appetite,
around our girl devotion has raptured past
starvation, her round face blank as a cookie
with gumdrop eyes, blind as a living doll's.

MANHATTAN

You've got to have a little faith in people,
the girl says, blinking tears. She's seventeen,
the wise, shy center of a film where couple

after couple split, East Side lovers blown
round an unending storm, while past them whirl
parks, cafés, planetariums. The screen

(she's sobbing) swears by Woody Allen's smile
like lead anchoring a cathedral window.
It's Chaplin's awful grin to the blind girl,

joy raptured from our grasp, Gershwin's crescendo
opening our eyes to what we're really kissing.
Moral child, your course new-bent for England, you

ache with your old man's treachery, his messing
up human fates on this small island. Granite
shifts underfoot, yet you tell this guy, piercing

your heart (again), *Have faith!* Faith! Who could want it,
some other silly girl, some other planet?
Oh brave new world that has such people in it.

WEAR

The birds wear air
and the fish wear water.
Once we knew
the soul wore matter
but now, no matter,
the soul wears down.
The duckling's down
lets it wear water
in wearying weather.
The weather wears
the sun's fire
that warms the earth
in its wrap of air.
Earth wears the moon
and the moon wears water,
pulling the tides
from their coastal harbor
and wearing them down
upon the sand
where the tides wear land,
where we wore each other
like winter clothing.
We watched our breath
and into the ground
we wore each other,
honeymooners
on a train
squabbling over
the lower berth.
Christ, how can you
lie, my darling,
naked under
cover in the winter,
wearing earth?

ABOUT the AUTHOR

Jay Rogoff's six previous books of poetry include *The Cutoff*, his Washington Prize–winning sequence, and, from Louisiana State University Press, *The Long Fault*, *The Art of Gravity*, *Venera*, and *Enamel Eyes*. He has also published two chapbooks, *First Hand*, winner of the John Masefield Award, and *Twenty Danses Macabres*, which earned the Robert Watson Prize. His poetry and criticism have appeared in many publications, and he also serves as dance critic for *The Hopkins Review*. Born in New York City, he has been an upstate New Yorker for his entire adult life and lives in Saratoga Springs.

www.ingramcontent.com/pod-product-compliance
Lightning Source LLC
Chambersburg PA
CBHW030540230426
43665CB00010B/969